Consider the Eel

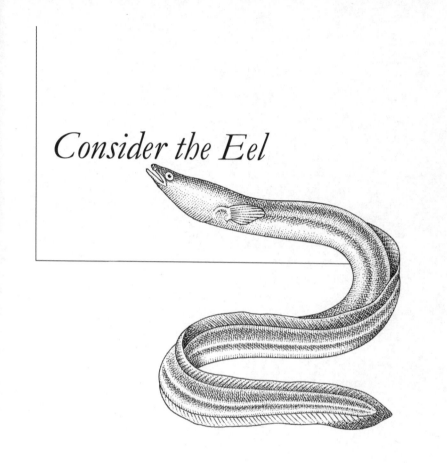

Consider the eel

RICHARD SCHWEID

The University of North Carolina Press Chapel Hill & London

This book was published with the assistance of
the Blythe Family Fund of the University of
North Carolina Press.
Designed by Richard Hendel
Set in Monotype Garamond
by Tseng Information Systems, Inc.
The paper in this book meets the guidelines for
permanence and durability of the Committee on
Production Guidelines for Book Longevity of the
Council on Library Resources.
Library of Congress Cataloging-in-Publication Data
Schweid, Richard, 1946–
Consider the eel / by Richard Schweid.
    p. cm.
Includes bibliographical references (p.) and index.
ISBN 0-8078-2693-6 (cloth: alk. paper)
1. Anguillidae. 2. Eel fisheries. I. Title.
QL638.A55 S38 2002
597'.432—dc21   2001048067

06 05 04 03 02   5 4 3 2 1

"Eel Pye with Oysters"
recipe reprinted from *A
Tryon Palace Trifle* from the
Collection of the Tryon
Palace Historic Sites and
Gardens. Excerpt from
"A Lough Neagh
Sequence" by Seamus
Heaney reprinted from
A Door Into the Dark
(London: Faber and Faber
Ltd., 1969) by permission
of the publisher, and from
*Opened Ground: Selected
Poems 1966–1996* by Seamus
Heaney, © 1998 by Seamus
Heaney, by permission of
Farrar, Straus and Giroux,
LLC.

Drawings © 2002 by
Ed Lindlof

For my brother David,
both friend and family

Contents

Preface *xi*

1 Pamlico County, North Carolina *5*

2 Interstate 95 *31*

3 Guipúzcoa, Basque Country, Spain *56*

4 Lough Neagh, Northern Ireland *81*

5 Yankee Eels *111*

6 Fishing and Farming *132*

   A Taste of Eel *154*

   Bibliography *161*

   Acknowledgments *171*

   Index *173*

How mobile, fleet, and uncontroll'd,
Glides life's uncertain day!
Who clings to it, but grasps an eel,
That quicker slips away.
—*Konrad Gesner (1516–65)*

Preface

It was a June morning in 1998 when I first learned some of the basic facts of an eel's mysterious natural history.

Every European and American freshwater eel is conceived and born in the weedy Sargasso Sea, a vast, rarely traveled, 2 million square miles of deep Atlantic Ocean between Bermuda and the Azores. The prevailing currents carry the larval eels to their prospective homes in the freshwater rivers of either the United States and Canada or Europe. The tiny larvae—shaped like little leaves—drift with the currents for about a year if they get carried to North American rivers, or up to three years if they are carried to Europe.

When the eel larvae enter fresh water, they begin to actively hunt food for the first time and transform into what we know as eels. They may live their bottom-dwellers' lives in fresh water for as long as 20 years. Then, one day, they head back downriver toward the ocean and begin to transform again, as their bodies prepare for what may be a journey of as much as a thousand miles across the Atlantic. Their digestive systems atrophy, because during the trip through the ocean depths they will rely on stored energy and will not eat. Their eyes start to widen, changing for optimal vision in dim blue ocean light, and their muddy-green bellies turn snow-white. They will encounter multiple predators during the long saline passage ahead, back to the Sargasso Sea, where they will mate, reproduce, and die.

I learned all these things in El Palmar, a small town just south of Valencia, Spain, and the eeler who explained the animal's life cycle to me did so as he served up an eel he had just taken from a trap, killed, cleaned, and cooked in olive oil in an earthenware dish. I ate it with a chunk of fresh, crusty bread. It was delicious. I was immediately fascinated.

That was, of course, just the beginning. The more I learned about the eel, the more I came to appreciate its biological and gastronomic qualities, both of which have fascinated people for millennia. It is a rich and fatty fish, high in lipids and proteins, with its own delicious taste. People seem to have always eaten it. Eels fed the Greeks in Aristotle's day, 2,300 years ago, and helped the *Mayflower* Pilgrims to endure their first year in North America in 1621. They are one of the human race's survival foods, and continue to be consumed in great quantities around the globe, prepared in a wide variety of ways. Although they have fallen out of favor in the United States, well over $2 billion a year is spent on eels in the rest of the world.

We are not talking here about the infamous electric eels of the Amazon and Orinoco Rivers, or the vicious moray eels that spend their lives in salt water. Neither of those eels is in the same family as the eels that North Americans and Europeans catch in their lakes and rivers. The life of an eel in the fresh waters of the Northern Hemisphere is a story of the mysterious wrapped in the commonplace. What could be more prosaic than an eel burrowed in the mud at the bottom of a creek, river, or lake? It seems a most ordinary life — eating, swimming, and resting. Yet, each of the millions of eels has come hundreds, or even thousands, of miles across the Atlantic Ocean to live in that little bit of muddy, freshwater bottom, and will make the trip in reverse before dying. Eels have never been bred successfully in captivity, nor are they known to have reproduced anywhere outside the Sargasso Sea.

As I searched for information about them, I began to have the occasional opportunity to watch eels, and the more I did so, the more I came to admire their grace of movement, their pure sinuosity. I found that I could observe them gliding through the water for a long time without becoming bored, and I came to agree with William Roots, a physician and naturalist from Kingston, England, who wrote in 1832: "The undulating motion of the eel in swimming is beautifully seen in watching these young creatures—indeed the whole process of their natural history is well worth much and patient observation."

I learned that there is an eel world with interlocking capitals around the globe, set like a palimpsest on our idea of the global consumer economy. Instead of being linked by cities like New York, Paris, and Tokyo, the global eel market is knit together in villages and towns like Arapahoe, North Carolina; Aguinaga, Spain; and Toomebridge, Northern Ireland. These are places where the eel is not an invisible resident or a casual meal, but a part of the base economy, directly connected to the lives of many of the people there.

Wild game in the world was long ago reduced to levels far below what is needed to feed large groups of people, but fish—the seas so vast, the piscine populations so large—began to disappear in significant numbers only in the last half of the twentieth century, when floating vacuum cleaners under a number of flags sucked available stocks to market for the few short years it took to seriously deplete or destroy them. The resource is disappearing, and will, apparently, be replaced in our diets by fish raised in captivity, perhaps genetically identical to their cousins in the wild, or perhaps genetically modified, but which, in either case, simply will not taste the same as animals that grew up foraging in seas, rivers, or lakes. An ever-growing number of fish bought and sold in the world is aquacultured, farm grown, and, if things continue apace, the great bulk of global fish consumption will come from aquaculture within a few decades. Fish caught in the wild will be expensive and scarce, perhaps providing a "free-range," or "organic," upscale market. It will soon be as hard to be a self-employed, independent fisherman or fisherwoman in the developed world, as it has already become to be a small-scale working farmer.

People who still fish for a living often see this state of affairs as a result of too much government interference in how they practice their craft. Strict seasons, catch limits, and licensing requirements are the bane of the workaday world on the water. But overfishing and environmental degradation, both profit driven, are far more likely culprits than governmental efforts to conserve stocks. Whatever the reasons, the world will be a poorer place when people are no longer able to earn their daily bread by fishing.

Juvenile eels can be caught and fattened to market size, but they cannot truly be farmed because they will not reproduce in captivity. Wildness is still a precondition to propagating their species. In an era when the very chromosomes of most of the things people like to eat, from salmon to corn, are being counted, catalogued, and altered, most aspects of basic eel biology and behavior remain complete mysteries.

As I find with all good subjects, the more I studied eels, the more there was to learn. In the end, it seems there's never enough time to include everything. That's life. A lot slips by. For the things left out of *this* book, I ask pardon by invoking the words of George Brown Goode's introduction to his monumental eight-volume study of East Coast fisheries in the United States, published in 1884, the likes of which has not been compiled since. If it was true for him, how much more so for me: "The fishery industry is of such great importance, and is undergoing such constant changes, that a visit of a few days or weeks to any locality, even by the most competent expert, has invariably proved unsatisfactory. We were able therefore to collect only the most important facts, selected by special reference to the needs of the report in contemplation, leaving many subjects of interest undiscussed."

Amen.

Consider the Eel

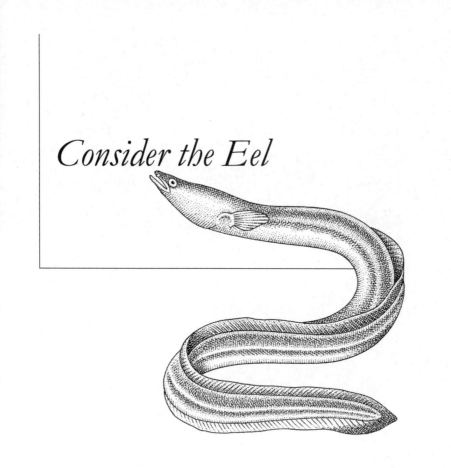

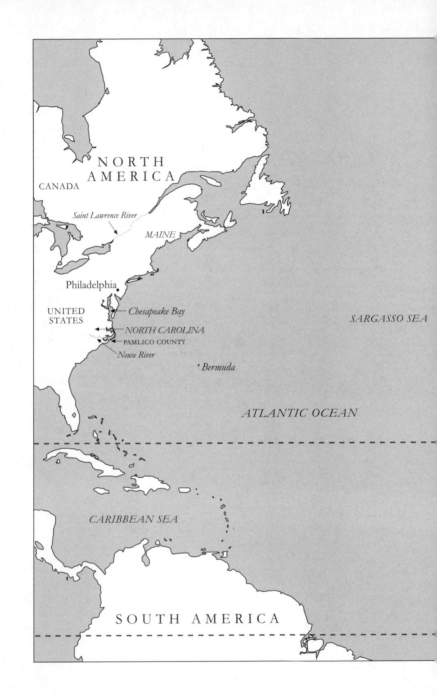

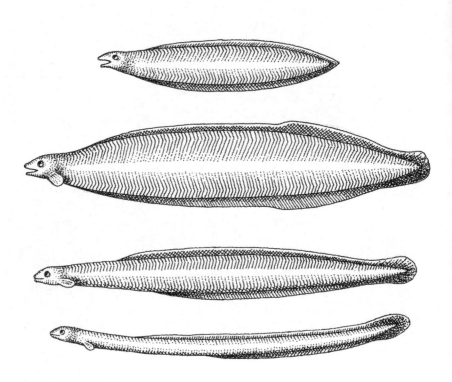

Development of the eel from larva, or leptocephalus (at top),
to elver, or glass eel (at bottom).
Drawing by Ed Lindlof, after Johannes Schmidt.

CHAPTER I

Pamlico County, North Carolina

"Watch Out for Bears" reads the black-and-yellow, diamond-shaped traffic advisory sign at the start of a 20-mile stretch of eastern North Carolina's four-lane Highway 70, a paved corridor with tall timber on either side. A confused black bear ambling out of these woods for a moment at twilight is not an unusual sighting. More common still, on roads all over the eastern part of the state, are deer, which can instantly ruin the front end of a car as they come bounding out of the night onto a highway and into the headlights; in a split second, a crumpling fender sends their hundred pounds or so flying through the air. What happens to the people inside the car will be a lot less severe if their seatbelts are fastened. And, of course, there are the smaller, although nevertheless startling, nighttime crunches and bumps of a racoon caught beneath a tire while running across the pavement, a rambling possum likewise flattened, or an owl, misjudging its altitude, clipped by the roof to tumble as a lump of cooling feathers to the side of the road. During the day, mostly snakes and tortoises are squashed into the asphalt.

Even when the car is not being assaulted by animal bodies, a person driving the roads of coastal North Carolina has a sense of being pretty far out in the wilderness. That 20 miles of bear-posted avenue through tall woods is just west of New Bern, a small city that was the second town incorporated in colonial days, in 1710, and served intermittently as capital of the colony, and later state, of North Carolina until 1792. These days, it is simply the seat of Craven County, home to a population of about 22,000, along with a pair of shopping malls, some lovely colonial houses, and the same beautiful frontage on the Trent River that it has always enjoyed. It is also, as it has always been, the last urban outpost before heading east into deep coastal country.

A few miles past New Bern is the eastern edge of Craven County and westernmost boundary of Pamlico County. From there, it is 26 miles by two-lane road through flat woodland and cultivated fields to the land's edge at the brackish water of Pamlico Sound. For long stretches on those backcountry coastal roads one encounters no other cars in either direction. Traffic is so sparse that drivers of vehicles passing in opposite lanes wave at each other. There may be an occasional house, or a mobile home up on blocks, and lots of long vistas of fields gleaming white with cotton or green with soybean plants, but there is hardly any sign of human habitation other than ploughed and planted ground. Every so often, one passes a family cemetery with a half-dozen headstones in a small, cleared plot cut out of the pine woods next to a house. Many miles of fields and forest, and other than worked ground there is precious little sign of human beings, certainly nowhere a person could stop and spend money. Urban America seems a long way away indeed.

While it may look like mostly solid ground from a passing car, no part of Pamlico County is far from big water, and always close at hand are the wild tracts of bogs, swamps, and wetlands that lead to the sound, or to the rivers that empty into it; there are many ambiguous, squishy square miles of neither land nor water but some combination of the two, hospitable to little more than alligators, spiders, mosquitoes, snakes, and the area's watermen, who know from long experience how to steer their boats along the narrow channels of open water that wind through the marshes of *Spartina* grass. Pamlico County encloses 341 square miles of land and 235 square miles of water. In the whole county there is only one stoplight—in the middle of Bayboro, the county seat—although there are half a dozen Holiness Pentecostal churches, and another raft of Free Will Baptist congregations, in addition to the usual Southern Baptist, AME Zion, United Methodist, and other black and white Protestant houses of worship. There are more churches than stores.

People living in this world of woods and water are both nourished and limited by it. It provides them, in many cases, with the means to make their livings and connects their lives to a traditional natural order. On the other hand, those who want to get in their cars and go see a movie, shop for clothes, or go to much of a mall will have to drive at least as far as New Bern to do so. People's lives near the coast are still shaped and bordered by the huge, wild, unpopulated space around them. There is no large industry, and many of Pamlico County's approximately 12,000 residents make their livings from the sound, whether by directly harvesting its fish and shellfish or by working in a crab house or seafood packing plant. Most of the rest of them work the land, farming soybeans, cotton, or peanuts.

Pamlico Sound is some five miles wide in places and extends 40 miles out to the barrier islands of the Outer Banks. It is a vast body of shallow, brackish water fed by the Neuse and Pamlico Rivers from the west and the salt water of the Atlantic Ocean that manages to flow into the sound between the islands of the Outer Banks from the east. It has traditionally been one of the nation's richest fishing grounds, much like the Chesapeake Bay of Virginia and Maryland, a few hours' drive to the north. Despite a continuing degradation of its waters, the sound was still, in 1999, a major source of blue crabs, winter flounder, shrimp, menhaden, mullet, and eels.

This blend of salt and fresh water has always provided income and food for people with traps, nets, and small boats, and there is still money, of a sort, to be made. A large number of the white men living in small Pamlico County towns like Arapahoe, Oriental, Bayboro, and Vandemere make all or part of their livings on the water, and the same has been true since the first Europeans settled here in the mid-1700s. New Bern, in neighboring Craven County, has always had its share of millionaires, particularly in colonial times when access to the sea made some maritime traders wealthy, but in Pamlico County people have never gotten rich, only gotten by, and counted themselves lucky, at that, to do so. Those black men from Pamlico County who managed to be their own bosses usually worked the land, farming and raising livestock. The occasional African American has fished commercially since slavery times, but as a rule black fishermen have been few and far between. Although most white men also farmed some and raised a little livestock, many of them made their primary livings on the water. They called themselves watermen, as they still do. In truth, there have always been a goodly number of waterwomen, too. The daughters of watermen sometimes took up fishing, and numerous wives have kept their husbands company, working in two-person teams through many a long day and night on the water.

"I'm a waterman," Billy Truitt, 71, told me. "I'll fish for almost anything. Crab, shrimp, oysters, speckled trout, you name it. I'm a waterman. My father was a waterman, and my wife Lucille's father was a waterman, too.

"My daddy was a mullet fisherman; that's what he did the most of. 'Josephines,' we call mullets here. He had six of us young 'uns to feed, and we had mullet ever' morning of our lives for breakfast. We didn't go hungry 'nary a morning."

Billy Truitt fished for a living since he was ten years old, when he decided that taking a skiff out on the sound and trotlining for blue crabs was easier than working in his father's corn field after school and on Saturdays. Over the course of his life, he owned three good-sized shrimp boats with inboard engines, as well as a variety of skiffs with outboard motors. His wife, Lucille Styron Truitt, who was also raised on the water by her father, was Billy's first mate for many years, and often his only on-board companion. When I met him in 1999, he was semiretired, setting nets a few days a week to make a little extra money, while Lucille stayed home minding their secondhand store in Oriental, a coastal town of some 800 people.

Other than shifting to nylon for a netting material, Billy Truitt fished in essentially the same way as had other fishermen thousands of years before him. The technique could not be less high-tech: set a few hundred yards of net held up by a handful of tall stakes one evening and pull it up early the next morning. The net makes a wall in the water and whatever swims into it overnight gets enmeshed. Gillnetting, pure and simple. The fish often die in the net before it is pulled, so there's no leaving it in the water during the day— after the sun comes up it does not take long for the meat to go off-flavor. That is why gillnetters are on the water at first light, hauling in their catch.

I pushed Billy's 12-foot fiberglass skiff, with its 25-horsepower outboard motor, off his boat trailer and into the sound at 5:30 one cool October morning. As he leaned out of the cab of his pickup, keeping a foot on the brake, he shouted directions back over his shoulder to me as I tried to perch on the trailer with the boat's bow line in one hand, using the other hand to push the boat down toward the water, with me following right behind. "Watch out, watch out, stay up on the trailer," Billy shouted, exasperated, as he watched me lose my footing and step down into the sound. The water poured in over the tops of my rubber boots, and I would spend the morning with wet feet.

The sky was lightening to a pastel rose above the liquid black of the Pamlico Sound's surface; the only night left above was a crescent moon and the morning star. An occasional early-rising seagull passed overhead, between us and the rose sky, an inky silhouette of body and outstretched wings. We motored out along the bulkhead that holds the sound back from Oriental, around the diminutive Whitaker Creek Island with its stand of loblolly pine, to a 14-foot-high bamboo stake that marked one end of Billy's set where he had laid down his nylon gill net, at dusk, the previous evening. Between the stakes, corks bobbed every foot or so at the top of a wall of net, which was weighted at the bottom with lead beneath each cork. The stake marking the other end of the net was barely visible, sticking up against the sky 500 yards away across the water.

Billy, wearing yellow oilskins, cut the engine and prepared to go to work. His formerly red hair was now mostly gray, though it remained thick, and his body had a rounded slope to it, but even at 71 he was a strong man who looked like he could hold his own. "I'm about give out now, I'm all stove in, but I used to be able to really work," he told me. "I could fish all day and all night."

He got right to it, standing in the stern, back straight, legs apart, one freckled, pale, square hand pulling in the cork line, the other the lead line, piling the net carefully at his feet so that it would go out smoothly when he set it again that evening. As the fish came in, he made quick work of disentangling and culling them. He was hoping for an abundant take of speckled trout (known elsewhere as weakfish), spot, croaker, and mullet, the species for which the fish houses were willing to pay. A couple of the speckled trout that came up in the net were big beauties, three pounds of flashing sea-silver bodies with black spots, lean and mean, with razor sharp teeth. These he handled a little more carefully, but the rest of the net's contents—trash fish or those it was against the law to keep—he got out as quickly as possible, pulling, pushing, ripping, and tearing them loose, throwing back the small flounder, hog chokers, puppy drum, and menhaden to swim away if they were alive or otherwise to sink, spiraling slowly, slowly, down, or be snatched off the surface by the gulls hovering in the air around us. Some of the fish in the net were nothing more than head and backbone, the meat all picked away by blue crabs or torn off by eels. The eels swim through or around the net and are gone by the time it is pulled, but the crabs frequently come up entwined in it. Billy broke their claws off, so they could not nip him, before disentangling and tossing them back into the water to swim off and begin the process of growing new claws.

The waxed cardboard boxes on the floor of the boat filled slowly with fish. It took Billy nearly three hours to run the net. He worked steadily, stopping only once to turn and relieve himself over the skiff's side. By net's end, his yellow oilskins were covered with fish blood, scales, and dirt from the sound itself. Hurricane Floyd had passed through eastern North Carolina the month before, with devastating results, leaving the water of the sound a reddish, rust brown, full of runoff from upriver pig farms, the dirtiest Billy said he had ever seen it. The net was piled waist high in the stern in front of him; the sun was well up in the sky; and there was occasional traffic on the water—crab boats pulling up pots, trawlers headed toward the Outer Banks, yachts with engines and yachts with sails. Billy dug two cans of Diet Pepsi out of the little red cooler he had brought with him, along with a pair of cellophane-wrapped packets of crackers and processed cheese. He sat down on the stern seat to eat this breakfast, the first seat he had taken in three hours, and he stiffened up so quickly that five minutes later, when we were done eating our snack and ready to head in, he had to spend half a minute gathering himself before he could lurch to his feet with a groan, yank the outboard's starter rope, and set the boat toward home under the blue sky and risen bright sun. At $1.50 a pound for the morning's 24 pounds of speckled trout and 50 cents a pound for the 50 pounds of mullet, Billy had spent three hours earning not much over $60, without even subtracting the cost of the gas and the soft drinks. Still, for three hours' work that came to pretty good money for a 71-year-old fisherman.

Boats on trailers seemed to be in almost every Pamlico County driveway. Pickup trucks were as common as cars, and a pickup without a boat trailer hitch was rare. A person with a boat could pretty well make a little money fishing all year long. Many people did. In the winter, there was oystering and pound nets to set for winter flounder. Then there were shrimp to be trawlnetted in the late winter and early spring. There was crabbing from late spring through mid-fall, and a person could always fill in by setting pots for eel or nets for speckled trout. The hurricane, and the subsequent heavy addition of river water and washed-away land into the sound, did not seem to have affected the blue crab population. Crabbers were reporting good catches and prices were generally high. North Carolina's blue crab landings are among the highest in the nation. There are a half-dozen crab houses in Pamlico County that buy blue crabs, which they steam in bulk and pass on to a room full of women, some of whom pick the meat out of the shells, while the rest pack and label cans of crabmeat.

There are a lot of similarities between crabbing and eeling, and many crabbers become eelers before crab season begins and after it ends. Baited traps, which are called pots, are used to catch both animals, although those for eel are smaller than those for crab. The tasks involved are much the same—hauling aboard a pot, emptying out its catch, rebaiting it, and tossing it back overboard. A North Carolina eel pot generally has two canvas funnels in it, the first leading into the pot and the second into the part of the trap where the bait is located. By the time the eel has gotten through the second funnel into what is called "the parlor," where the bait is located, it cannot find its way back out.

The blue crab is an animal adapted to brackish water, moving back and forth between high and low salinity over the course of its life cycle, all of which is spent in the sound and the ocean right around it. The eel, on the other hand, is only passing through on its amazing journey. It is extraordinarily curious looking, one of the most unlikely of fish. Shaped like a serpent, it has small gills in front of a pair of tiny fins, and a long fin on top running almost the length of its body, ending in the semblance of a tail. Its slimy, mucous-covered skin is made up of tiny scales, which are virtually invisible, so small that ancient rabbis judged it to be without scales and therefore deemed it nonkosher, prohibiting its consumption.

The life cycle of eels has fascinated and baffled observers ever since it was first commented on by Aristotle around 350 B.C., in his *Natural History,* and much of it remains as unknown today as when the first great naturalist wrote about it. Aristotle correctly observed that eels live in both salt and fresh water and that, unlike most other fish that do so (such as salmon), they migrate from the sea to rivers instead of from rivers to the sea. In fact, it is now believed that the eel and the mullet—Billy Truitt's "Josephines"—are the only two North American fish that do this, making them catadromous, in scientific terminology, unlike salmon and all other species that live in salt water but are born and reproduce in fresh water, which are known, scientifically, as anadromous.

Eels, as food, were held in high esteem by the Greeks, so it is not surprising that Aristotle had a go at explaining eel reproduction. Eels were unique among all creatures, he concluded, because they have no sexual organs and are not produced from sexual intercourse, but are spontaneously generated from mud. He got it wrong, but he was only the first of many. Aristotle was no further away from the truth than the eminent naturalists who followed him down through the centuries. Almost all of them felt obliged to have their say about the reproductive behavior of eels, and almost all of them were wildly wrong.

Pliny the Elder asserted, around 60 A.D., that eels reproduced by rubbing their bodies against rocks, with the small flakes of skin they shed becoming baby eels. Oppian, a Greek naturalist in the second century A.D., thought eels copulated by rubbing together and generating the slimy coating that makes them so slippery:

Strange the formation of the Eely Race,
That know no Sex, yet love the close Embrace.
Their folded lengths they round each other twine,
Twist am'rous knots, and slimy bodies joyn;
Till the close strife brings off a frothy juice.
The Seed that must the wriggling kind produce.
Regardless they their future offspring leave,
But porous Sands the spumy drops receive.
That genial bed impregnates all the Heap.
And little Eelets soon begin to creep.
Half-Fish, Half-Slime they try their doubtful strength,
And slowly trail along their wormy length.
                                        (trans. John Jones, 1722)

It was a perfectly reasonable hypothesis. The slime covering an eel's body *does* look like it might be some sort of sexual secretion, but biologists now know it is generated by glands in the skin to serve two principal purposes—it gives an eel the capacity to survive longer out of water than most fish, and it protects against bacteria—but the mucous has nothing to do with reproduction. Not all the great naturalists made such reasonable assertions as Oppian's, but all offered their considered opinions on eel reproduction, and they were all convinced they were right. Since no one could definitively prove how eels reproduced, no theory could be wholly discounted.

In fact, more than 2,000 years after Aristotle, things were still not much clearer when Sigmund Freud was attending medical school at the University of Vienna. His first independent research task, for which he was given a grant and time for a few weeks of research at a zoological experimentation station in Trieste, Italy, was to search for eel testicles. It was a far cry from the subconscious, although the male eel's gonads were almost as well hidden. Eel reproduction was one of the burning scientific research issues of the day, and Freud's work was supervised by Carl Claus, the head of the university's Institute of Comparative Anatomy. The paper that the future father of psychoanalysis wrote about his research, in 1877, was titled *Observations on the Form and the Fine Structure of the Looped Organs of the Eel, Organs Considered as Testes.* In it, Freud explained, "No one has ever found a mature eel—no one has yet seen the testes of the eel, in spite of innumerable efforts through the centuries." He was unable to conclusively locate the eel's testes but did believe he had found them, and later research would prove him right. He was not happy that the results of his work were less than definitive, but it would be some time yet before much more was understood about eel reproduction. Not until after the First World War did these mysteries really begin to be unraveled, although the male gonads had been conclusively located by the end of the nineteenth century, right where Freud thought they were.

The known facts, as they are pretty much universally accepted among biologists and naturalists today, are that all the eels in all the rivers of eastern North America and the Caribbean countries, and all the eels in all the rivers of eastern and western Europe, are born in the same area of the Sargasso Sea, a huge area within the Atlantic Ocean, between Bermuda and the Azores, the surface of which is frequently covered with sargassum seaweed. In fact, the word "Sargasso" comes from the Portuguese *sargaço,* meaning seaweed. The sea is about 2,000 miles long and 1,000 miles wide, set off from the surrounding waters of the Atlantic by strong currents. It includes the area known in popular legend as the Bermuda Triangle.

Eels hatch in the Sargasso as larvae and are carried by the ocean currents to either Europe or the United States, a journey that can cover thousands of miles and take years. Where they end up depends on which of two similar species they belong to. Those that are *Anguilla anguilla* invariably wind up in European rivers, and those that enter North American rivers always belong to the species *Anguilla rostrata.* The first person to find eel larvae in the Sargasso Sea was Danish researcher Johannes Schmidt, who published his findings in 1924, after spending 18 years hauling nets in search of eels.

The larvae of both species are shaped like small oval leaves and are called leptocephali. Each leptocephalus begins to assume the form of a tiny eel, called an elver or glass eel, when it gets close to the coasts of either Europe or the Americas. By the time it reaches brackish water, where fresh and salt water mix, it is thin and transparent, hardly bigger than a hair, with a pair of eyes like black dots at one end.

From the estuaries and mouths of rivers, the tiny eels frequently continue upstream, particularly the females, who sometimes go great distances inland. American eels have been found as far up the Mississippi River system as the rivers of Iowa. They keep going upriver until something tells them they've reached home, and then they stop. Whatever it is that signals to eels that they are home is definitive—they settle in and live there for as long as 20 years, growing up to a yard long before beginning their journey back to the Sargasso Sea. Scientists determine an eel's age using a microscope to read the growth rings of its otolith—a small, hard calcium deposit at the base of its skull.

In preparation for the return journey to the Sargasso, sexually mature female eels feed voraciously and change color from the muddy-yellow/green of adult eels, often called yellow eels, to a darker green on top and snow-white on their bellies. At this stage, they are called silver eels. They swim downriver in the fall, on the first leg of their journey to the Sargasso, and when they reach estuarine waters, they rest, completing their final transformation as silver eels. They will have eaten heavily and will be about 28 percent body fat. They will never eat again, and their digestive systems will atrophy. Their pupils will expand and turn blue. They will need a new kind of sight adapted to the depths of the sea, where there is little light. They will also have to go through a drastic adjustment, called osmosis, in their blood chemistry, to prepare for the tremendous change in water pressure, going from some 14 pounds of freshwater pressure per inch of their bodies to over a ton of ocean pressure per inch. Once they are back in the Sargasso Sea, the females produce eggs for the males to fertilize, and then the adults die.

At least, that is what today's marine biologists and naturalists tell us, although adult eels have never been seen swimming, reproducing, or dying in the Sargasso. In fact, live adult eels have never been seen there at all. The only two adult eels ever reported in the Sargasso Sea were dead, found in the stomachs of other fish. The eel's migration back to its birthplace and what it actually does when it gets there are assumed to take place far below the water's surface and, as of the year 2001, are still completely unobserved. However, the eel larvae—the leptocephali that Schmidt found in the Sargasso—were so small that it was certain they had been born recently, and nearby. Such small larvae have never been seen elsewhere, and while eels have never been observed reproducing in the Sargasso, they have never been seen doing so anyplace else either. Scientists believe the larvae hatch out of eggs at a depth of 100–300 yards and rise slowly toward the light at the sea's surface.

To the naked eye, European and American eels are indistinguishable. The only visible difference between the genetically distinct species is that the European eel has 114 vertebrae, while its American cousin has 107. The meat of both species tastes nearly the same—a rich, pure fish flavor that can be delectably prepared in a great many ways. Eel is respected, and in many cases prized, as food all over Europe. It is consumed in the greatest quantities in the northern part of the continent—in Scandinavia, the Netherlands, Belgium, Germany, France, and England—but is also eaten frequently in Mediterranean nations like Spain and Italy, as well as in eastern European countries like Hungary, Bulgaria, and Poland. Total eel consumption in northern Europe alone is around 22 million pounds a year, according to *Aquaculture Magazine*.

Despite vast expenditures of time and money in the effort to get them to do so, eels steadfastly refuse to reproduce viably in captivity. The Japanese have harvested eggs from females and fertilized them artificially; larvae have been hatched, but they would not eat and quickly died. The person who is eventually successful at reproducing eels that will eat and thrive in captivity stands to make a lot of money: in 1995, according to government figures, Japanese consumers purchased about 190 million pounds of eel, worth roughly $1.8 billion at that year's exchange rate. As it is, large facilities where baby eels are fattened to market size exist in a number of countries, including China, Japan, Denmark, Holland, Italy, and Spain, but all the eels they raise were born in the wild and captured shortly after they turned from larvae into young eels. Well over half a billion pounds of eel are thought to be eaten each year around the world, and it all comes from wild stock. In addition to everything else that is not known about eels, it is unclear whether the development of a juvenile into a male or a female is wholly genetically determined, as in most other creatures, or is dependent on other factors as well, although it is not known what exactly the other factors might be. In short, never has an animal been studied for so long and eaten in such quantities, yet remained so little known.

The Sargasso Sea is likewise mysterious. It is home to such legends as that of the Bermuda Triangle, into which ships are said to have disappeared with alarming frequency, and the almost equally infamous horse latitudes, where months pass with little wind, and where the horses aboard the becalmed ships of early European explorers were driven crazy by thirst and were said to have leapt—or been pushed by sailors eager to conserve water—into the sea. The Sargasso is the deepest part of the Atlantic, where both underwater continental shelves, that of North America and that of Europe, slope down to a wide valley floor almost 4,000 feet below the surface. Some marine biologists have postulated that eels were originally born here when Europe and North America were barely separated by water, or even joined by land, and that as tectonic plates shifted and the continents drifted apart, the eels continued to return to the valley to mate, even as the journey for both adult fish and newborn larvae grew steadily longer and more hazardous.

The Sargasso is well out of the shipping lanes, and because fish are relatively scarce in its tremendous depths it does not attract fishing vessels. It is one of the emptiest, least-known parts of the world, and it is vast. It is shaped like a roughly drawn oval, and the strong currents that define its borders move it slowly in a clockwise direction. Strangest of all, perhaps, are the thick mats of sargassum, seaweed that appears floating on the surface of the sea, then disappears, hundreds of miles from shore. It is buoyed up by floats that look like amber grapes among the weed. The sargassum reproduces when the tips of its branches break off and float away to form a new clump. There are a handful of animals that live in the weed, small fishes and crabs and such, but there is relatively little marine life in the Sargasso.

The weed at times appears in isolated patches and at other times in mats stretching virtually from horizon to horizon. The first European to report it was Christopher Columbus, in his journal, on his way to the New World. His entry for Sunday, September 16, 1492, records: "We have begun to see large patches of yellowish-green weed, which seems to have been torn away from some island or reef." The next day he dictated to his scribe: "I saw a great deal of weed today—weed from rocks that lie to the west. I take this to mean that we are near land. . . . Some of the weed looks like river grass and the crew found a live crab in a patch of it. This is a sure sign of land, for crabs are not found even 240 miles from shore." Columbus wrote this as he crossed into the eastern edge of the Sargasso Sea, with well over a thousand miles and many more days of watching the weed still ahead of him.

Eels are, as they have always been, there for the taking in many rivers of the eastern United States and Canada. Almost every state with rivers that empty into the Atlantic has some commercial eel fishing. North Carolina has an active, if modest, fishery, with over 100 people annually reporting commercial sales of eel at the end of the twentieth century. In 1997, some 129,000 pounds, worth over $325,000, were reported as commercial landings in the state, and most knowledgeable observers say about half of the landings and sales go unreported, so annual eel sales in North Carolina are probably well over $.5 million. Even the state's reported catch made it the third largest in the nation, trailing only those of Maryland and Virginia. Almost all of North Carolina's eels, as well as Maryland's and Virginia's, were bought by one of three East Coast brokers who turned around and shipped them by air, alive, to customers in Europe.

Early European settlers, and the Native Americans before them, ate a lot of eel. It was among those foods that Tisquantum, the Pawtuxet Indian who took pity on the bumbling, Bible-beating white settlers, taught the *Mayflower* Pilgrims how and where to find, pointing it out as one of the staples in the New World larder. Among those early comestibles were a number of indigenous American foods with which the Europeans were unfamiliar, some of which, such as lobster, they ate only when there was nothing else available; eel, however, was a perfectly familiar food to them, something that their ancestors in England had been eating for centuries.

As early as 1066, the *Domesday Book* mentioned that Evesham Abbey had an eel fishery on England's Severn River, which yielded as many as two thousand eels at a time. In the fourteenth century, a passage in *Piers of Fulham* decries the growing custom of killing small eels for their livers and discarding the rest of the animal as being too young to cook. Eel was a staple in the earliest English cookbooks, and people were eating it well before forks were introduced into England in the mid-1500s by a traveler who saw the utensil in Italy and carried the idea home. The earliest printed recipes were for dishes that people would eat with their fingers, so sauces tended to be thick and ingredients large enough for a person to grasp. In what is thought to be the earliest English-language cookbook, *The Form of Cury,* which was probably compiled between 1370 and 1400, there is a recipe for an eel pie, easy to eat without a fork. And in *A Noble Boke off Cookery,* another of Britain's oldest cookbooks, written about 1460 by a chef to the household of an unidentified prince, there is a recipe for pike and eels in broth, which begins with a bit of doggerel: "Pik and eles in ballok brothe / that muste our dame haue or els she will be wrothe."

The hungry British colonists who first settled North Carolina were as happy to see eels there as the Pilgrims had been to find them in New England. John Lawson, England's first surveyor-general for North Carolina—he died at the hands of Tuscarora Indians in 1711 at one of the tribe's villages along the Neuse River—published a book in London in 1709 called *A New Voyage to Carolina.* It was the first book describing this part of the New World to those who had stayed behind and was intended not only to describe the new lands but also to promote them as a good place in which to invest. Lawson catalogued and lauded Carolina's natural resources and the ease with which sustenance could be taken from its wilds. "Eels are no where in the World better, or more plentiful than in Carolina," he wrote.

That is still, arguably, the case today, but despite their abundance in the state's coastal rivers, most North Carolinians will not eat them. Those who do so either have highly eccentric culinary tastes or are dirt poor. Some old-timers remember the days when store-bought meat rarely graced a table, and it is from those hard times that the few local recipes for eel have come down. They are simple preparations, designed more to get the meat cooked and on the table than to prepare it with careful attention to either flavor or presentation. The most frequently found way to cook it is as fried eel or, occasionally, a rudimentary eel stew.

Eel is virtually no longer consumed by people in the United States, the end result of a long decline in popularity that began after the Civil War, while in Europe its value as a food product has been steadily rising. These days, Europeans eat about 25,000 metric tons, or 55 million pounds, of eels each year, and they are willing to pay good money for them, including those from North Carolina. The market fluctuates, depending on the size of the native eel population during any given season. Wild eel landings have dropped by nearly half in Europe over the past 25 years, and while more European eels are being farmed, there is always some market for American eel.

Unlike diners in Paris, who do not blink at paying $25 for a plate of eels—served as an eel *matelote* or, perhaps, *anguille au vert*—most contemporary North Carolinians would rather drink muddy water than eat an eel, regardless of how it is prepared. They share the attitude exhibited by Lucille Styron Truitt when I offered to fry some for her and Billy for supper one night: "I never would eat one. Looks too much like a snake."

Lucille, a short, solid woman at 72, spoke her categorical refusal to sample eel from the depths of an armchair set squarely across from the woodstove in the middle of her store. Her pronouncement carried quite a bit of weight with me, because she had already put things on my plate that I had never sampled in more than 50 years of eating three times a day, and then some.

Lucille would feed a person on a moment's notice, as if the dozen years she had worked as a waitress in the now-defunct Oriental Marina Restaurant had left her with an unbreakable habit of putting down food in front of folks. A visit to her store often included an invitation to sit down near the stove and let her bring you something to eat from her kitchen, and that something often turned out to be new to the taste buds of the invitee. Within a month of our acquaintance, she had fed me, at various times, her homemade pimento cheese with olives, persimmon pudding, pickled green tomatoes, rutabagas, and collard greens in a one-pot dish with lean ham and corn meal dumplings (the best collards I ever ate in my life), which she said her mother used to cook a pot of every day.

Billy Truitt and I got back from a fishing expedition one morning about 9:30—we had shoved off at dawn—with some 35 pounds of speckled trout, a bunch of roe mullet, and some spot, which to my tongue is the tastiest of the fish caught in the Pamlico Sound. It had been a sunny, calm, productive morning, and everything went pretty well. I had pushed the boat off the trailer without getting water up over the tops of my boots, so I had the pleasure of dry feet all morning, and I didn't screw up too badly standing next to Billy in the stern and pulling in my side of the net—the lead line with its lead weights, to be sure, rather than the cork line, which required a defter hand—as we tossed back black drum, white perch, puppy drum, fatback (menhaden), croaker, hog choker, undersized flounder, and juvenile striped bass.

When we got back to the store, Lucille had collard greens ready and waiting for us. Coleslaw on the side and a Diet Pepsi out of the store's refrigerator made a breakfast that just hit the spot. I ate and ate, until I was stuffed, satisfied by a good day's work, although it was only 10:00 A.M.

"Hey," said Lucille. "Did y'all hear about the new restaurant that's serving possum? There's a line out the door; families showing up with their young 'uns, everybody wanting some. Didn't y'all hear about it?"

"No," said Billy and I, simultaneously. An addition to Oriental's restaurants, where dining opportunities were limited, was big news.

Lucille waited a couple of beats. "Well, what they do is, first they put the possum on a board and put sweet potatoes around it, and then they bake it for half an hour; then they take it out of the oven and throw away the possum and eat the board."

She laughed, hard.

Lucille's place of business was identified by a sign as The Ol' Store, and it had a nice, broad front porch with a half-dozen rocking chairs lined up side by side behind the railing, each different from the others, where a person could rest and rock among the geraniums set out in coffee cans, fish nets with old-fashioned handmade corks on them, bent tools, piles of newer nets that were waiting to be mended by Billy, and an ever-changing assortment of odd bric-a-brac. From the rocking chairs, one could idly contemplate the Fulcher's Seafood plant across the narrow street, where some 125 imported Mexican workers, mostly young women, spent eight months a year, March through October, picking and packing crabmeat. Or nod at sailors walking by in front of the porch, on their way up to town from the public dinghy dock. Oriental, located on the Intracoastal Waterway, is a favorite stop for people in sail and motor yachts going north and south. There is a substantial boat traffic in the fall heading toward Florida, and in the spring heading back north. The town billed itself as the sailing capital of North Carolina, and its otherwise scant commercial roster included three sailmakers although there were no stores selling dry goods and there was only one grocery store, which was out of town on the main highway. Two groups of people were often seen making the trudge out to the supermarket: the sailors, often middle-aged couples in shorts and Timberland boat shoes who had walked into town from the dinghy dock wearing expensive backpacks to fill with the provisions they intended to buy (and found it was a good hike along unshaded Highway 55 to reach the store), and short Mexican women in T-shirts and long skirts, with their hair pinned up, carrying nylon shopping bags, wearing rubber thongs on their feet.

The public dock was just a short block away from The Ol' Store, so people who rowed their dinghies to shore from their yachts and walked through town would pass by Lucille Truitt's place of business. "More museum than store," was how she described the long, high-ceilinged, dimly lit wooden building where she sold decades' worth of accumulated secondhand stuff, everything imaginable, from radios to toasters, T-shirts to place mats, at rock-bottom prices. The Mexican women working across the street found the store's prices and stock of North American castoffs much to their liking and frequently came in when their shifts were done to search through the store's shelves.

When Lucille was a little girl, her father, Clyde Styron, fished full time. She was an only child, and the first years of her life she spent each spring during the shad runs living with her mother, Gertie, and father aboard a flat-bottomed houseboat, which they anchored wherever there were fish. The rest of the year her father fished for whatever was in season. Once Lucille was of school age, however, the family stayed closer to land. Her father opened a general store at the Oriental harbor, and Lucille came in off the water to live ashore and go to school. That was when she first met her future husband, Billy—in the first grade. When a fire destroyed her father's original store, he opened a new one in 1950, where The Ol' Store now stands. Then, in 1958, her father announced that life was too short to spend it all working inside, and he nailed up the store's windows and doors and went back to fishing. The store stayed closed until 1975, when Lucille and Billy decided to reopen it.

Lucille's father died in 1969, after a slow decline during which she helped her mother nurse him. It was a dark, depressing time for her. Whenever Lucille talked about her parents, it was easy to tell how much she still missed both of them, to hear it in her voice and read it on her face. She took after her daddy in a lot of things. He was a fisherman and later in his life a storekeeper, and she followed the same path, punctuated by the birth of her son and two daughters and the years she worked as a waitress.

She began painting while tending her father and found that it helped relax her, and that her father loved to see her scenes of Oriental in the old days, painted from her vivid memories. Lucille discovered that she had a real talent for painting, and she kept it up after her father died, particularly in the winter, when life was slow and quiet. In January and February, the woodstove was kept stoked, and Lucille stayed in the store and painted. Her canvases of life in Oriental, and on the sound, had gained her a certain reputation as an outsider artist. Her work hung in homes as far away as New York. She only painted in winter—in summer, she said, there was not enough uninterrupted time. Billy and Lucille kept a small apartment at the back of the store, and the business had no posted hours. It was open when either or both of them were at home, and not open if they were someplace else.

When the store *was* open, winter or summer, people gathered there, a wide range of people. A day's visitors might range from yacht owners who passed by Oriental every year, always anchored overnight, and stopped in at the store for a twice-yearly visit, to local people with whom Lucille went to grade school ever so long ago, who still lived in Oriental and came by the store a couple of times a week to pass a while with her. Everyone dropped by for essentially the same reason—the pleasure of Lucille's company. She always kept a few chairs for guests around the woodstove in the middle of the store, was an accomplished raconteur, and was completely open to the possibilities offered by strangers.

"Sit for a spell and tell me about yourself," she would invite visitors to the store who looked like they might have a good story, or who might just enjoy listening to Lucille tell one from her own inexhaustible supply. She was a deep well of information on a multitude of aspects of life in Oriental. But when it came to eels, all Lucille could say for sure was that they had always been around and she knew that some people were reputed to enjoy eating them, but she had never seen anyone actually doing so, and would, herself, have to be downright starving before she would even consider sampling them.

Lucille's friend Captain Billy Mason, who was 97, tall, thin, frail, and slow, told me he remembered hearing about an Oriental man named George Midgyett shipping eel north by train as early as 1895. And Lucille did remember watching her daddy pack eels in barrels and put them on a train to Baltimore in the mid-1930s, when the train still ran through Oriental. Billy Truitt remembered using chunks of cut-up eel as bait for his crab trotlines in the mid-1950s. The blue crabs liked eel better than anything, he recalled. You could buy chopped-up pieces of fresh eel cheap. Even though he was using them for bait, and was a waterman through and through, he never fished for eel: "Just never took to it."

There were plenty of others who did take to it, however. Among them was Ann Braddy, for instance, who expected to grow old and die without ever tasting eel, but who certainly caught a lot of them during each year's pair of two-month eel seasons, one in the spring and one in the fall. Braddy lived near Belhaven, some 30 miles north of Oriental as the crow flies across Pamlico Sound, and she spent four or five months each year running 200 eel pots every morning. She rose at 4:00 A.M. and was on the water at first light. Her 18-foot skiff was all open deck, pure workspace, no place to sit down. She steered standing at a battered console in the middle of the boat, which was powered by a 75-horsepower outboard, and when she came to a float marking one of her pots, she threw the boat into neutral and pulled the pot in. A North Carolina eel pot is a rectangular trap made from galvanized wire coated with plastic. There is a canvas funnel at one end, and a latch at the other so it can be opened when pulled aboard to dump the catch into a big, blue barrel on the deck, and then rebait the pot. For bait, Braddy used blue crab, horseshoe crab, shrimp heads, or trash fish like menhaden, known locally as fatback. She was convinced that blue crabs worked best, and not just any blue crab but females recently killed and put in the eel pots with their backs cracked open. Just as blue crabs are drawn to eel chunks as bait, so eels love freshly killed blue crabs. When Braddy shook the eels out of the pots, all that was left of the crabs were hollowed-out shells, with not a shred of meat inside. An eel pot is not heavy and is usually fished in only about six feet of water, so she did not have far to pull each pot, but 200 of them over the side of a boat every morning was hard work.

At 51, Ann Braddy did it alone, and loved it. Of course, she was a woman who during crab season set out 500 crab pots, also pulling them in by hand, and she claimed to love that, too. The mother of six children—five girls and a boy, all of whom have attended the local Christian academy—she was short, fit, and attractive, with curly blonde hair, sparkling blue eyes, and the ruddy, weathered face of someone who had spent a lot of time headed into the wind in an open boat. She had square, ready, rough hands. "With each of my children, I fished right along until I was ready to give birth. Then afterward, I'd bring the baby out with me on the boat, keep them in a crab box right on the deck. I've got to be so sick I can't even crawl before I won't come out."

She and her husband, Wayne, each had a boat, and each fished full time. Together, they also owned a small crab house, L & B Seafood, across from their home, where they would buy crabs from other fishermen and ship them out to customers. The family lived in a low, sprawling ranch house at the edge of Pungo Creek, which runs into Pamlico Sound. Ann Braddy's father was a waterman, and it wasn't until she began to try to find her place in the working world that she realized how much the water meant to her.

"The first place I went to work was in a crab company office, then in the office of a Honda shop, and then in an office at the hospital, but it just weren't the water, if you know what I mean," she told me, very early one morning, as we loaded boxes of "sooks"—female blue crabs—onto her boat before going out to pull and rebait her pots. "I said to myself, 'I like the water more'n I like people.' And, I decided to fish for a living. I was out crabbing for about a year before I got brave enough to reach in and get eels out of the pots myself. I was helping my husband run his eel pots on his boat, and at first I thought of them as snakes and didn't want to touch them. Now, I'd rather eel than crab. If it's good, the pot's full and it feels like you're doing real good. Those are great days, but you get them less and less."

Once we were on the water, she was all business, brusquely refusing my offer to help pull pots, and gave me to understand that my job was to stay out of the way and not distract her. "These days I'm lucky to get 300 pounds of eel in 200 pots, while it used to be that I have got 600 or 700 pounds. Most of the time now, if you have six eels in a pot, that's good."

The sun rose while she was pulling up pots. It was a late autumn morning, and the eel season was just ending. She was wearing orange oilskins, a baseball cap with "L & B Seafood" written across the front, and a dirty pair of white rubber boots. She moved efficiently about the deck, driving the boat, pulling the pots, dumping the few eels they held into the big blue barrel, and rebaiting. She sipped from a plastic mug of coffee balanced precariously behind the steering wheel on the console, and she hardly spoke until we got back to the dock and the eels had been transferred from the blue barrel into a wooden underwater cage chained to a piling. They would stay there until an eel dealer came by with a live-haul truck to buy them. "Well, you see how it is. I'm not getting enough in those pots to make it worthwhile. It's time to pull my pots for the year. The season is just about done. It's time to go gillnetting in the creeks for mullet and do a little oysterin' if there's any this year. Eel season's been okay, but it's just about done."

That was okay with her, she confessed, because deer season had only just begun the day before, and she was itching to get out in the woods. Hunting season begins in Pamlico County, as everywhere, when harvest season ends. "I went out yesterday and cut down the brush that's grown up around my deer stand, getting things ready for the season. I don't really go out there for the meat. I like venison, but I never even take my annual six-deer limit. I could if I wanted to — I've always got my gun with me when I go out there — but I won't shoot young males, or does, or anything except mature, racked males. The young does and males I see, and I see a lot of them, I just watch them.

"The woods at dusk — now there's something I dearly love. You're in the stand by yourself, but you're never lonely. The birds are coming in for the night, and the foxes are coming out. I've seen bear and deer feeding in the same field together, which is something most people say never happens. Most people live a whole lifetime and are never lucky enough to see that."

Bear-sighting anecdotes of one kind or another grew more frequent as the fall advanced in Oriental. In mid-November, bear season opened. The local newspapers published stories reminding readers that there were thousands of bears in the area and that in the previous year there had been 102 incidents of cars hitting bears in eastern North Carolina. Legislators were proposing that a series of culverts be built beneath main thoroughfares like U.S. 70 so that bear and deer could go under, rather than across, the highways. In the meantime, drivers never knew what might be about to come out of the woods onto the road in front of them. The bears were so numerous that there were two brief hunting seasons, one lasting about a week in mid-November and another of similar duration in mid-December.

John Lawson, in 1709, had high words of praise for the meat of North Carolina bears, which he described as "nourishing and not inferior to the best Pork in Taste." These days, if any part of a shot bear is used, it is the skin, which might be saved for a rug or wall trophy. Even the skin may not be used, however, and most of the meat is thrown out, nothing more kept than a photo of the dead bear spread out in the dirt, men in camouflage clothing and blaze-orange hunter's caps kneeling beside it, each with a rifle grasped in one hand.

A lot of towns I encountered down east in North Carolina consisted of nothing more than a post office and a mini-mart/gas station, at the approximate center of a scattering of houses with prefabricated siding and tin roofs or mobile homes with weeds grown high around the concrete blocks they rest on, looking battered and old, with rust stains beneath the window frames and aluminum skirts bent. Some of the mini-marts had a sign out front: Bear Weigh Station. Alongside them there was occasionally a parked pickup with a few men at its back, holding rifles, boots up on the truck's lowered tailgate, looking down at the truck bed and a pile of black fur with a rictal mouth, pink tongue lolling death-slack between yellowed teeth. Behind me in the supermarket line in Oriental, a guy with a six-pack of Miller and a big bag of potato chips, a tall, older man, said he and his friend had each killed a bear the day before — they had weighed 300 and 450 pounds, respectively.

"Well," Billy Truitt said, in a less-than-convinced voice when I told him the story the next afternoon, as we sat rocking on The Ol' Store's front porch, "I'm not saying it's not true, but those would be pretty big bear. You usually don't see them too much over 150 pounds. My friend Benny came by here yesterday with one in the back of his truck weighed just about 150 pounds, I'd guess. His dog got it up out in the woods. I helped him carry it on over to Bayboro. He wanted to get the head mounted. I don't know why. There's plenty of bear out there. Most ever' day when I'm out at my deer stand I see one. I could shoot a lots of them, but why do it? I'm not gonna eat bear, and I don't see the point to killing them."

CHAPTER 2

Interstate 95

Speak the words "eat" and "eel" in the same sentence, and, like Lucille Truitt, most North Americans will grimace at the thought of consuming such a snakelike creature. But the reaction of Europeans, particularly those from Martie Bouw's native Holland, is quite different. They generally salivate, and reach for their wallets.

That cultural distinction was what put Martie behind the steering wheel of his 18-wheeler on a Maryland stretch of Interstate 95 one October morning, hauling a refrigerated trailer with 6,600 pounds of boxed live eels that were late for their flight to Italy from the Philadelphia airport. He had bought those three metric tons of *Anguilla rostrata,* the American eel, over the past couple of weeks from more than a dozen eelers, including Ann Braddy, who had trapped them along the estuaries of North Carolina, Virginia, Delaware, and Maryland. Martie Bouw (pronounced *bow,* as in "take a bow") spent part of each week with a live-haul trailer hooked up to his new Volvo truck, traveling back roads in those Mid-Atlantic states and buying eels. Up and down the East Coast, eelers with hundreds of pounds of live eels in underwater cages awaited his visit.

He brought the eels to a half-dozen big concrete tanks, with well water constantly running through them, beside his rural home outside the small town of Arapahoe, some ten miles west of Oriental. Martie, his British wife, Marie, and their three children lived in a house behind the Holland Seafood eel processing plant. To get there, it was necessary to drive a couple of miles down a dirt road and then turn onto a second, narrower, graveled stretch, alongside which were posted a succession of warnings: Private Property, Keep Out, Beware of Dog. The place was carved out of the loblolly pine woods that surrounded it, and another 50 yards behind the house was Bear Creek, a large pond-shaped body of water with a narrow neck leading to the Pamlico River, and beyond that to the sound. The creek lived up to its name. Already that fall, Martie had seen a black bear with three cubs not far from his house. It was a wild and lovely location, but he taught his kids to be cautious: over the course of most years he killed a couple dozen water moccasins just in the yard between the creek and his eel tanks.

Once the eels were swimming in Martie's concrete tanks, into which he pumped up to 4,000 gallons of water a minute from the same well that provided his family with drinking water, he kept them alive for a few days, not feeding them, giving them time to purge. Then, the live-haul rig was replaced behind the Volvo by a refrigerated trailer. The live eels were packed in waxed card-board boxes, each holding ten kilos (22 pounds), and the boxes were stacked on pallets, which were loaded into the reefer to be driven to an airport. Martie had kindly invited me to ride along with this particular load, which was eagerly awaited in Rome. Most of the eels in the boxes would survive the trip, only to end their lives a few days later on a dish in some restaurant, perhaps as *spiedini di anguilla all' isolana* or *anguilla arrosto.*

Philadelphia was some 500 miles from those concrete tanks in Martie's side yard, a long haul from the gravel driveway leading through the woods to his house, but it was the closest airport with a direct flight to Rome, and eels do not fare well if they have to change flights. These were smaller eels, and Martie was particularly glad to be shipping them. Most European customers wanted large ones: the Belgians wanted them big for dishes like *anguille au vert,* and the Dutch and Germans wanted big ones to smoke. The smaller eels were not in much demand except in Italy, where they were highly regarded. A good Italian customer was, therefore, valuable to a North American eel dealer. The three metric tons he was hauling had cost Martie $1.50 a pound, and Rome was paying $2.27, a markup of 51 percent, although the air freight and the truck's gas bill would take a big bite out of the profits.

Bouw, officially vice president and plant manager of Holland Seafood, was having a bad morning on that October day, because he had just found out that he had only 30 minutes to reach the Philadelphia airport or the airline would not accept his shipment to Rome. He was an hour away, even if traffic did not slow him down and he was able to push the big rig hard along the interstate. To be in Philadelphia with more than three tons of eels — over $9,000 worth — that he could not ship would represent a substantial financial blow to Holland Seafood, but the possibility was looming.

It was, in a sense, his own fault. At 10:00 A.M., under the impression that he had a 1:00 P.M. deadline at the airport, he had chosen to pull off the interstate at a truck stop in Elkton, Maryland, to get his rig washed. Bouw, 48, had been driving big trucks all his working life, for many of those years in Europe, and still spent a lot of time on the road, either buying eel or driving those he had bought to different East Coast airports.

"Fishermen," he snorted contemptuously, as he maneuvered the truck into the line of tractor trailers waiting to go through the truck wash. "I don't know how they do it. If I had to be working out on the water every day in a boat, I couldn't stand it. I've always liked being out on the highway. Give me a truck, anytime, and when it's new like this one, it's better yet."

He loved being part of the American trucker culture and seemed to bring to it the same sense of pleasure that a foreign baseball player might feel upon making it into the major leagues. He had reached the top level of truck driving, the U.S. system of interstate highways, where speed limits are flexible — unlike in Europe, where there is a governor on truck engines that keeps them from going above 110 kilometers, or slightly over 60 miles, per hour. Martie

Bouw is a handsome, silver-haired Dutchman with blue eyes and a trimmed white moustache who spoke fluent but heavily accented English. He liked to kid around and was known and liked by the personnel at his favorite truck stops. These were the kinds of places that had telephones mounted on the partitions between booths so that tired-looking drivers wearing denim and cowboy boots and wide belt buckles, eating breakfast at any hour of day or night, running on trucker time, could use the phones to call their wives and bosses. Martie, sitting in front of a plate of steak and eggs, talking on the phone in Dutch to an eel wholesaler in Holland, had a voice that stood out above the general background hum and thrum of conversation, plates being set down, and country music. He did quick pounds-to-kilos conversions on a calculator beside his plate with one hand, while holding the phone with the other. He joked with the waitresses and left good tips. Even among the diverse faces in a big East Coast truck stop, Martie's was notable.

He was inordinately proud of his new, top-of-the-line Volvo, which had set him back about $100,000, and he was glad to spend $62 and a full thirty minutes inside the Blue Beacon Truck Wash waiting for it to be gone over from top to bottom by five snappy young guys wielding high-pressure hoses. The chubby young blonde woman behind the cash register greeted him as a regular customer. On the wall behind her was a plaque naming the Elkton franchise as the 1996 Blue Beacon Truck Wash of the Year, and a sign that read "We Drug Test." Tractor and trailer gleamed when Martie pulled out into the sunlight, admiring the truck's shine in his big side mirror and proudly asking me, riding shotgun, if it didn't look good. "Cheap at the price," he said. "It would take me three hours to wash it myself, and it still wouldn't look this great."

As Martie was driving away from the truck wash, the cell phone on the dashboard squealed. It was his wife, Marie, calling from their home in North Carolina to say she had just heard from the airline. They had called to make sure he knew his deadline had been moved up to 11:00 A.M. Martie cursed bitterly and began to worry. We moved into the left-hand lane of Interstate 95 and headed north, while Marie began some long-distance negotiating with the airline from Bear Creek.

American eel have been traveling to Europe on airplanes since another Dutchman, George Robberecht, moved his family from Holland to Nova Scotia in the early 1950s. There, much to his surprise, he saw fishermen throwing eels away as trash fish. Robberecht also saw a New World business opportunity. He went through Canada's eastern provinces, buying eels and freezing them for transportation by ship to Europe. After a few years, he read about the Chesapeake Bay and decided to move his operation there. By the late 1950s, his company, Robberecht Seafood, had shifted to buying live eels and sending them back to Holland as airline freight.

In the 1960s, half a dozen other seafood dealers along the East Coast followed Robberecht's lead and began selling to Europe. They were willing and eager to send live-haul trucks to North Carolina for eels, and there was a flurry of interest in the early 1970s on the part of the state's marine bureaucracy, which briefly saw eel fishing as an industry with lots of growth potential. The enthusiasm did not last long, but for a while North Carolina's Division of Marine Fisheries, in conjunction with the federal Sea Grant program, encouraged fishermen to branch out into eeling. There were low-interest loans to buy equipment, and Sea Grant even made a half-hearted stab at reinvigorating a culinary appreciation for the eel. A booklet about the harvesting, handling, and marketing of the animal, published by the program in 1975, gives a handful of recipes at the back.

It appeared, briefly, that eel was on an economic, if not a culinary, roll, and it looked like North Carolina might have itself a significant new source of revenue—but it did not happen. It quickly became clear that the resource was limited. Practically no sooner had large numbers of fishermen taken Sea Grant's advice and turned to eeling, than the number of eels rapidly fell beneath the level needed to keep the industry on a growth curve. Jess Hawkins, an executive assistant with the North Carolina Division of Marine Fisheries, remembered how it was in the early 1970s: "I grew up around here and saw a lot of the young people I came up with go into eeling to supplement their income. At the time, it was very profitable, a very high-dollar fishery. People made a lot of money. Then, beginning in the mid-'70s, the Sea Grant program began encouraging people to get into the fishery.

"They fished out the Pamlico and Neuse Rivers. We saw a decline of the fishery starting in the mid-'80s and a lot of fishermen shifted out of eeling. The eel takes a long time to mature, and once it's in a stream it's in that stream and is susceptible to being fished, and the eel pot is a very effective way to fish for them. The fishery simply went past the carrying point of the system and they overexploited the fish."

Before it became clear that the eel population would not support a large commercial fishery, many observers thought the state was on its way to being a strong player in the international eel market, and, in the mid-1980s, some Dutch investors began Holland Seafood in Arapahoe. They sent over a Dutchman named Willy Bokelaar to run it. In 1989, Bokelaar was joined by Martie Bouw and his family. "When I came here there were a half-dozen dealers willing to come and buy eels and, even so, we could still pick up twenty tons a week," Bouw told me. "That has been going steadily down. Last week I bought about twelve tons and that's a lot for these days."

Willy Bokelaar left the company in 1995 to devote himself to eel aquaculture, and Martie has run Holland Seafood ever since, buying and shipping American eel to customers in Europe. The company used to have a husband-and-wife team driving the truck, but Martie saw an opportunity to cut some costs and do a better job himself. He liked driving and saw no point in paying someone else to do it. In fact, by the time I visited him, his only employee at the plant was one young man from Arapahoe who worked at doing whatever needed to be done in the cycle of keeping the eels alive—sizing them, packing them, and keeping the place hosed down and clean. Other than him, it was Martie and Marie who moved millions of

Anguilla rostrata across the Atlantic every year, managing the whole thing from down at the end of their dirt road.

By 1999, Martie was one of only a trio of eel dealers left on the East Coast, and the only one with headquarters in North Carolina. When George Robberecht died at the age of 85, his daughter, Wilhelmina, and son-in-law, Maurice Bosse, kept Robberecht Seafood running in Newport News, Virginia, but they operated on a small level and never threatened Martie's business. His only serious competition, he said, was a company in Philadelphia. His competitor was always looking to entice away his eelers, on the one hand, and his customers abroad, on the other. Martie bought eel wherever he could, ranging from a fisherman who lived in a house trailer with his family just down the dirt road from Holland Seafood, to Ann Braddy over near Belhaven, to eelers from as far away as Virginia, Maryland, or Delaware.

Even though North Carolina's eel rush was over almost before it began, in years when the harvest of eels from European rivers was poor, demand on the Continent was high and Holland Seafood still stood to make some good money. However, as Martie was always quick to point out, it was never *easy* money. An eel dealer had a worrisome and stressful job. He had to keep an equilibrium between the number of eels coming into the tanks and the number going out. It was not possible to wait until he had a customer with an order for a specific number of eels and then buy that number from eelers. When eelers were holding hundreds of pounds of eels in underwater cages, they did not want to wait long for someone to come get them. When an eeler called to ask Martie to come get a load, he had to go buy them and keep the eeler happy. It was not the eeler's problem if Martie did not have anywhere to turn around and sell them. Fishermen were a fickle lot, he said, and many of them had left him when his competition offered them a few cents more per pound. Then, even worse, they would think nothing of calling him again when his competition would not come for a load of eels.

"That's the kind of fisherman they were talking about," he explained, "when they made up the joke: 'Don't worry if a fisher-man's sleeping with your wife; at least it means your boat's safe.'" He laughed bitterly, behind the big steering wheel of the Volvo, as our hydraulically engineered seats gently rose and fell with the bumps in the highway and the miles rolled away beneath the eighteen wheels. "Then, when they call me to ask if I'll come buy a bunch of eels they've got, I tell them to call my competition, even though I know damned well the only reason they're calling is because the competition has already said they don't want them."

Eelers in down east North Carolina frequently live way out in the country. They like to mind their own business and expect other people to do the same. The work they do is possible only for an independent-minded person, and they value their privacy and soli-tude. They often arouse a certain antipathy among those who go to work for someone else each day, pay their full taxes regularly, and make the daily, life-consuming trudge toward retirement.

In 1843, J. C. Bellamy wrote a book for the women of England, *Housekeeper's Guide to the Fish Market,* about shopping for fish: where, what, and how to buy. Beware the unsavory fisher, he warned house-keepers about English fishermen, who might well have been ances-tors to some of those reclusive, coastal North Carolinians. (Down east coastal Carolina speech, even today, is laced with the accents and intonations of England.) Bellamy complained: "As respects the moral and political condition of fishermen in general, I must record that both are of the worst possible description, strongly demanding investigation."

Martie Bouw might not have put it in just those words, but he felt as if he had endured more than his share of deception and ill treatment from eelers, and, for that matter, from his European cus-tomers as well. "It's not just the fishermen who screw you. For in-stance, my customers can deduct so much for every dead one if more than 10 percent of the eels are dead when they unload them from the plane, and when they do, I don't have anyone there to tell me if they're lying. Then, too, there's the competition. They're always calling up my customers and offering eels at 25 cents a pound less than me; they're willing to lose money to put me out of business. When you're talking about tons of eels, 25 cents a pound can be pretty tempting. I have some loyal customers, but the competition would love to see me lose them."

He never called his competition by name. "A Philadelphia Jew," he answered, when I first asked him just who "the competition" was.

I told him I was Jewish myself.

No offense intended, he assured me.

Some weeks later, driving through the tiny town of North East, Maryland, having just bought the day's first load of eels before it was even fully light, after we had gotten to know one another better, he told me about his father. We had slept a few hours in the truck, parked at a truck stop among the other rumbling 18-wheeled pachyderms, Martie in the lower bunk and me up above. Then, as the sun rose, we drove down to the North East River, behind an Episcopal church where the riverside cemetery in the churchyard was covered with golden leaves from the shedding maple trees that shaded the gravestones. We were met at water's edge by an older man with a paunch and a white beard, wearing a dirty white T-shirt and blue jeans, and his two young helpers, both wearing waders. They hauled the eel cage out of the water and up a boat ramp so the animals could be dipped out and loaded in the live-haul trailer. Mist hung over the river, and a flock of Canadian geese came to life, honking, rising off the water's surface behind the graveyard. The older man told me that for 20 years he had been eeling, as well as fishing this same stretch of river for catfish with fyke and pound nets.

We loaded up some 800 pounds of eel, and as we rumbled back through the empty, early morning streets of the picturesque little town, something made Martie think about his father. "He was one of the largest cattle farmers in Holland. He was a hard man. He was sent to Auschwitz during the last six months of World War II for helping to print the newspaper for the Dutch resistance. He was healthy, so they kept him alive to work. He spent those months stacking the bodies of Jews ten feet high as they came out of the ovens, after the gold was yanked from their teeth and their fingers cut off for their rings.

"He didn't talk much about what he went through, but when people started saying the Holocaust never happened, he told me they should have been there and seen what he'd seen, and he told me some about it."

After half an hour stuck in slow-moving, northbound traffic on I-95, as he imagined the United Airlines flight taking off for Rome without his eels, Martie was building up a full head of worry. What was he going to do? If they had been big eels, he could at least have taken them back home and kept them in the tanks until he found a northern European customer; but what was he going to do with three tons of small eels if they missed the flight? In the middle of all his worrying out loud, he was interrupted by the high-pitched tone of the cell phone erupting on the dashboard. It was Marie calling to tell him he could take it easy; the airline had agreed to let him pack and ship the eels whenever he arrived.

Once we got there and had the trailer backed up to the loading dock, it took us an hour to off-load the hundreds of boxes of live eels and stack them in the airline's five-foot-high cargo container. While they weighed only 22 pounds apiece, by the end of an hour lifting and stacking them, we had both broken a sweat. "A baby sweat," Martie said, disdainfully.

By 1:00 P.M. the truck was parked by a chain-link fence in the back of a vacant lot in the industrial park next to the airport, where the cargo terminal was located. A few hours' sleep in the bunk bed at the back of the cab, and he would turn around and drive the return leg to North Carolina. In a good year, Martie might sell $1.5 million of eel to Europe, which would leave him with a net profit of somewhere around $150,000. Other years, those that were not so good, he said he did not make enough to pay for the hours spent buying, selling, trucking, shipping, wheeling, dealing, losing sleep, and worrying through all of it.

"I don't know how much longer I can keep this up," he told me. "I like the work, but I have a family to support, and I just don't know how long I can do it by dealing eels. Every year it seems like it's tougher to make a living. This year I'm thinking about taking the truck during the winter and doing some cross-country hauling for other people. Produce, whatever, just rent myself and the truck out, and keep some cash coming in. I don't know. Marie and I have to sit down after eel season's over, look at the figures, and see if we're going to be able to keep doing this."

When the eel larvae near the end of their immense drifting journey and approach a coast, they transform and begin to look like tiny eels rather than willow leaves. The first person to document this remarkable change was the same scientist who first found them in the Sargasso Sea, the Dane Johannes Schmidt, who during the 18 years he spent towing nets all over the Atlantic looking for leptocephali, was able to photograph examples from each stage in the metamorphosis. As elvers move out of salt water and into brackish, estuarine water, they are tiny, transparent ribbons; wriggling through the water, they look like nothing so much as small, see-through worms with a pair of tiny black eyes at one end and a thin, dark lateral line running from head to tail. In this stage, they are often referred to as glass eels, presumably because they are transparent. A high tide will carry them into the mouth of a river, and they will begin to ascend it in great numbers. Within a few days of being in fresh water, the elvers will take on a muddy, dark pigmentation.

In countries where eel is eaten in large amounts, the ability to provide elvers in fixed quantities of a reliable quality can be highly profitable. In Europe, China, and, most of all, Japan, eels can be raised to eating size and sold again for a profit. While eel farming is not practiced in the United States, it is a serious business in other places. Elvers are the seed for these farmers, and as such they are often, quite literally, worth their weight in gold.

The nation that consumes the most eel is Japan, where approximately 200 million pounds are sold annually. The Japanese freshwater eel, *Anguilla japonica,* is believed to be born in an area of the Pacific Ocean similar to the Sargasso, and the larvae are delivered to the rivers of China, Korea, and Japan by the Kuroshio current. While the numbers of elvers entering the rivers of the United States and Europe went into a slow decline during the 1990s, *japonica* elvers virtually disappeared. The Japanese prefer *japonica* to either the American or European eel, because it is fatter and more flavorful, but it is not such a different species that they will not settle for the others if *japonica* are scarce, and that is what they have been doing for a number of years.

Eels have been farmed in Japan since the end of the nineteenth century, but fish farming space in a small, populous country like Japan is at a premium, and there is simply not enough acreage to grow enough eels to satisfy demand. Eel farms growing product for the Japanese market appeared on Taiwan in the 1980s. Mainland China, with its vast farmlands and much larger production capacity, got into the act in the early 1990s and has become Japan's principal provider of eels.

A steady supply of elvers is the base on which the entire eel farming industry rests. Without glass eels, there is nothing to fatten to eating size. Throughout the late 1980s and 1990s, the numbers of *japonica* elvers dwindled, and the prices of European and American elvers skyrocketed. By 1989, the price of American elvers on the Asian market was upward of $400 a pound. Of course, a pound is a lot of elvers—some 1,500—but the prices continued to climb. American elvers were relatively plentiful along the East Coast of the United States, and people living along the eastern seaboard have long described the "walls" of glass eels that flowed into the rivers at high tide.

Buyers for Asian eel farms turned up on riverbanks all along the East Coast, with live-haul trucks and pockets full of cash, during the few weeks each year when elvers were entering the rivers. It is easy enough to catch elvers moving en masse by simply dipping a fine net into their midst and pulling it out. During some years, in elver season a person could make more money selling baby eels than selling heroin. Disputes over elver fishing territory were occasionally resolved with guns. A couple thousand dollars a night for a few weeks made the rest of the year easier to bear. One North Carolina elver fisherman remembered nights in the early 1990s when he got paid over $5,000 for a load of elvers, and no one asked him for a Social Security number.

For a little while it looked as if the slack of the declining adult eel fishery in North Carolina, and all over the East Coast, would be taken up by the elver fishery. For a very little while. Most states responded to a declining adult population by prohibiting elver fisheries. By the year 2000, there were only four states—Florida, South Carolina, Connecticut, and Maine—that allowed elvers to be fished in their rivers, and these fisheries were strictly regulated. Elver fishing in North Carolina was effectively prohibited in 1995, when the state enacted a six-inch minimum size limit for harvested eels.

Willy Bokelaar, Holland Seafood's original manager, who was both fishing and dealing elvers, strongly opposed the prohibition. He maintained, as have some academics and just about everyone who made any money from elver fishing, that the fishery did not significantly impact stocks and that if it was necessary to prohibit any part of the eel fishery, what should be prohibited is the taking of large, adult females on their way downriver as they head back to the ocean and the Sargasso to reproduce, because each of these gravid females represents upward of 2 million eggs. So far, the elver fishing prohibition does not seem to have halted the decline in the adult eel population, but it may be too early to tell, since eels generally take at least seven years to mature.

One thing most experts agree on is that a factor in the thinning of the world's eel stocks is deteriorating water quality. "The more I deal with eels, the more I come to believe that they are, essentially, just like humans," Martie Bouw said, as we ate a midnight breakfast at a Waffle House restaurant just off the interstate, the truck parked and idling outside. "If you want to understand something about eels, just look at how humans would react in the same situation.

"Look at this Waffle House, for instance. The food is good, and it's cheap, but the counters are dirty, the place isn't really clean. I'll eat here, but my wife would refuse. An eel is the same way. Water quality is everything to a baby eel looking for a freshwater river to enter."

No one can say for sure, but the general wisdom holds that where an elver decides to come to shore has nothing to do with where its progenitors spent their freshwater years. They are not thought to return to the same rivers where their mothers lived. The whole American eel population is one undifferentiated species, one gene pool sharing just the same needs, unlike, say, salmon, which can be genetically differentiated according to the river where they hatch and return to spawn. What factors *do* influence an elver's choice to bypass North Carolina and come inland at Maryland, or New Jersey, or Connecticut, or Maine is a mystery, although scientists believe a combination of factors—among them, water temperature, tide, and smells—is responsible. Whatever the reasons, there is no denying that North Carolina's river system, particularly the Neuse, has suffered a precipitous decline in quality over recent years and is surely not as attractive to an elver as it might be. The state is one of the largest hog producers in the nation, raising some 10 million a year, and the bulk of its hog farms are built on lowlands. There are an estimated 185 industrial-size pig farms in what is called the 100-year flood plain of eastern Carolina, which is the area that can be expected to flood at least every 100 years. It has happened more frequently than that in recent history, because development of various kinds has reduced the land's capacity to absorb water. When there is a breach in the walls of a lagoon in which hog waste is being stored, the resulting seepage or runoff of untreated waste ends up in the river.

The flooding that accompanied Hurricane Floyd, in 1999, was of the cataclysmic variety: 51 people were killed, 43,000 homes were damaged, and the rivers rose so high that when they receded eels were said to have been strung up in the tree branches like tinsel. The raging waters ruptured 4 hog waste lagoons and swamped 47 more. Hundreds of thousands of gallons of raw pig waste wound up in the Neuse, heading seaward. Also floating downriver as the waters receded were a good part of the 28,000 swine, 2,000 cattle, and more than 2.8 million chickens and turkeys killed by the hurricane. A number of marine biologists and environmentalists predicted a massive ecological disaster, including a dead zone in the estuaries that might resemble the one that extends from the Louisiana coast far out into the Gulf of Mexico. Fortunately, it did not happen. The water was filthy, but the levels of catch during the fishing, crabbing, and shrimping seasons remained normal. Apparently, the extra volume of water during the flood was enough to dilute the pollution caused by the same flooding.

The Neuse River has suffered decades of intense abuse as a dumping ground for industrial and agricultural garbage, as well as municipal sewage. Since the 1960s, it has gone through periods of being closed to fishing because of excessive amounts of everything from DDT to the extraordinarily toxic dynoflagellate *Pfeisteria piscaida*. What effect the chronically polluted water of the coastal rivers has on eels is, like so much else about the animals, little understood. The eel is a hardy fish, able to survive extremely low oxygen levels in its burrows in the mud, and there are numerous records of eels surviving large fish kills when oxygen levels fell below what was needed in a river or lake for other species to survive. Unfortunately, down in the mud is also where the heavy metals, pesticides, and herbicides settle after they run off the land. Little research has been done, but in one 1993 study of the European eel from Greece, the heavy metal cadmium was proven capable of causing irreversible eel liver damage, and in 1997 researchers working with the American eel in the St. Lawrence River concluded that organochlorine compounds could cause a variety of pathological changes to the animal's health. A handful of toxicological studies have found eels in rivers around the world with levels of PCBs (polychlorinated biphenyls) and dioxins far above the maximum recommended levels.

Pollution is not the only threat to the system of rivers and streams in which the eel passes most of its adult life. Many of these bodies of water are no longer accessible to eels because they have been blocked by dams or filled in by developers. Eels are relentless in their drive upriver, and it takes a lot to stop them. There are numerous reports of elvers scaling dams, using the dead bodies of those that went before them and remained plastered against the dam's face to scale the impediment. On damp evenings, eels are not averse to slithering long distances across land to go around an obstacle from one body of water to another, and enough people have caught them at it over the centuries to have created a substantial body of reports, as well as a bunch of good stories.

Edward Jesse, an Englishman, whose credibility as a natural historian is low, told one of the best in his 1834 volume *Gleanings in Natural History*, when he wrote about what he claimed was an annual occurrence in Bristol, England:

> Near that city there is a large pond immediately adjoining which is a stream. On the bank between these two waters a large tree grows, the branches of which hang into the pond. By means of these branches, the young eels ascend into the tree and from thence let themselves drop into the stream below, thus migrating to far distant waters, where they increase in size, and become useful and beneficial to man. A friend of mine who was a casual witness of this circumstance, informed me that the tree appeared to be quite alive with these little animals.

One of the few things that is known about eels is that they can live up to 48 hours out of the water, if there is moist, shady vegetation, taking in oxygen both through their gills as air and by "diffusion" through the skin. An eel is a fish for which land is no barrier, and its willingness to cross land means that it is sometimes found in lakes and ponds that have no communication with other rivers or streams, causing many to believe that the eels must have been born in that same place. Despite their persistence in moving forward, however, there are some dams too large for elvers to scale and housing developments too wide for eels to slither around. In the United States, the federal government estimated that eels had lost some 80 percent of river and stream access along the coastline of the eastern United States and Canada by the mid-1990s. Larger eels are not averse to eating their smaller colleagues, and overcrowding in the bodies of water that remain accessible may be contributing to the reduction in the numbers of eels.

Or perhaps the decline in catch numbers results from neither pollution nor destruction of habitat, but can be chalked up to the overfishing of elvers in the early 1990s, when prices for the juvenile eels were high, leading to a shortage of adults that is only now showing up. While neither the reasons nor the numbers can be pinpointed, it is pretty much agreed that something is reducing the eel population, and that there is cause for concern. There is a regulation in place specifying that all sales from eelers to dealers have to be reported to the National Marine Fisheries Service (NMFS), but it is generally accepted that compliance is low. Even taking underreporting into account, however, it is apparent that the population is declining. In 1979, one of the best years on record for American eel catches, over 3.6 million pounds were reported to the NMFS. Nineteen years later, in 1998, that number was about 900,000 pounds, or a decline of 75 percent. In 1999, the Atlantic States Marine Fisheries Commission decided to act. The commission sets regulations for fisheries in the fourteen states that have Atlantic coastlines, every state on the East Coast from Florida to Maine. Since the American eel comes from a single population, and elvers are just as likely to enter one river as another, what is done to benefit the eel population in any one place will eventually have positive effects on the whole population. By the end of 1999, the commission had created its first fishery management plan for the American eel.

Fishery management plans are not just so many more pages of reports and recommendations. They have the force of law, and a state failing to implement the plan's provisions can have its fisheries shut down by the Department of Commerce. The eel plan requires an annual report from each state detailing its regulations, harvest, and efforts to monitor its eel population. Fisheries officials hope, in this way, to assemble a picture of the basic numbers and conditions of American eel stocks. The plan was based on input gathered from state agencies that deal with commercial fishing, as well as from some eelers themselves.

In North Carolina, the hands-on eeler asked to put his two cents' worth into the management plan was Robert Hutchinson, 70, a transplanted Yankee from Medford, Massachusetts, with an accent straight out of South Boston, who lived in Chocowinity, a good 45 miles northwest of Oriental in Beaufort County. He had been eeling the waters of eastern North Carolina since he retired to the state in 1980. He was a square stump of a man, short, squat, barrel-chested, with a grizzled white beard, who had spent 30 years in the military working with explosives. He had to wear two hearing aids, if he wanted to have a serious conversation, but despite all those years around things that go boom, he still had all his fingers. Agile fingers they were, too. Robert Hutchinson could build just about anything. Those hands of his had put together boats, even cars, and hundreds of eel pots, not to mention his house, which was a big, comfortable, roofed platform raised way up on stilts. He lived there with his wife, Helen. An arm of Chocowinity Bay, off the Pamlico River, was on the other side of the road that passed in front of his house, and that's where he tied up his boat. He got up every morning, crossed the road, got in his boat, and went out to pull his pots. Hutchinson learned to eel from Billy Wychert, one of the area's early commercial eelers, and he set out a couple hundred pots a day during the season. Robert Hutchinson took the task of providing input to the eel plan seriously and put a lot of work into the section dealing with catch statistics.

When I went out with him to pull pots, he was wearing army-olive oilskins over a white T-shirt. He had the thick forearms and biceps of a man who spent a lot of time pulling things out of the water and didn't seem to mind all the hard work, the bending over a gunwale to snag a pot, the hauling, emptying, rebaiting, and tossing back of the same pot. "It's critically important to get accurate stock counts of eels from dealers and eelers, so that we can know how many eels are taken each year," he told me, taking a couple himself, which he dumped out of a pot and into the barrel on the boat's deck. "Look, from 1983 to 1987, we used to catch ten pounds a trap, and we were getting 50 or 60 cents a pound. Now, we're getting $1.50 a pound, but we're only getting two or three pounds in each trap. Man, 1983 was a fantastic year. We caught over a million pounds just here in North Carolina. We just plain overfished them.

"Add to that the pollution. 'Chocowinity' is an Indian word, meaning breeding ground for fish. Really, the whole Pamlico Sound is a breeding ground for fish, but Chocowinity Bay is about the only clean part left of the Pamlico River. It's fed by Chocowinity Creek, and now they've started a pig farm upstream, and we're starting to pick up some nutrients. No telling how much longer it'll stay clean.

"Something is negatively affecting the eel population, and we need to know what it is. In the early 1980s, in a radius of seven miles from here, there were 23 boats eeling regularly. Now there's only one: me. I'm retired from the military, so it's not my only source of income, but I'm a full-time eeler. I do it because I love it, not because I have to do it to get by. I enjoy eeling and it's exercise for me, but if you're going to make a living with eels, your whole living, you've really got to bust your ass."

That's what Gary Koonce did, and he made a living at it. He agreed that eels were scarcer in North Carolina than they had been a decade ago, but he believed they had started to stage a comeback. "It's tough work, but this 1999 season was a good one," he told me. "I've been eeling for more than 20 years, since I was 17. This year, I started off with about 150 pots, then moved right up to setting out about 300 pots a day, and next year I'm thinking to do 600. Between me and my daddy, we've been catching around 450 pounds a day in those 300 pots."

Koonce, 33, was of medium height with a rotund, fireplug build, light brown hair, blue eyes, and a couple days' growth of beard on a rounded, pleasant face. He was making eel pots when I stopped by to speak with him. He had his pot manufacturing operation set up under a grove of loblolly pines in front of his mobile home. The land had belonged to his family for three generations. The table on which he made pots had a roller mounted at one end, from which unspooled a big roll of galvanized wire. He could make 38 eel pots out of each roll, and a roll cost $250. Each pot, therefore, cost him about $6.50, while at the Belhaven Crab and Eel Pot Store, some 12 miles east of his trailer, eel pots sold for twice that much.

Like lots of eelers, he lived a long way away from anything much at all. The directions he gave me on the phone were typical of how to get to many an eeler's home. "Well, you come through town, then you take Jackson Swamp Road, then the paved road off to the right after a couple of miles, and after another couple of miles it's the sixth trailer down on the right side."

When I got there he was standing at the pot-making table, his left hand squeezing the meat at the base of his right thumb, out of which blood was slowly oozing. "There was a four-foot chicken snake in the yard and my mom wanted me to kill it," he explained, "but I didn't want to, so I just went to sling it across the road into the woods, and it bit me. That's gratitude for you."

He did not seem particularly worried or flustered about the snakebite. When he was five years old, his family moved "out to the country" from Bath, a town of a couple hundred residents. Many people would think of Bath as pretty much out in the country already, but where he was living on his family's land, traffic was heavy if more than a half-dozen cars drove past during the course of a day—and they would all be driven by people he knew. "I'm just a country boy. I've been to Virginia a few times, but I always thank God when I cross that North Carolina line again."

His best eel fishing of the year was for about three weeks in the spring, when the roe herring enter the rivers to spawn, ripe with eggs. Herring roe is at the top of the list of an American eel's favorite things to eat. The eels like nothing better than to come up under a ripe herring in the river and press their heads on the herring's anal vent, which causes the eggs to stream out. The Roanoke River, close to the Virginia border, is the site of an annual roe herring run, and a number of the eelers who normally work the Neuse and Pamlico

Rivers go up there to take advantage of it. The best thing about the whole situation, they say, is that the people who live around the Roanoke do not fish for eel, leaving the bounty to those who come from elsewhere.

"Jesus Christ almighty," Koonce marveled. "They're so packed in the pots up there you have to reach in and pull them out; you can't tip them into the barrel, they're so packed in. After half an hour in the water, your pot'll be slam-full. The fishermen up there will ask, 'Can you sell them eel? What are they worth?' We're up there fishing right in their back yard, and they don't even know what an eel pot is. It don't last long, but while them herring are there, man, that's some eel fishing. You can do 4,000 pounds in three days.

"They'll suck the eggs right out of those herring. You can just touch the belly and the eggs squirt right out. Ever' egg. You get a herring without any roe in her and you'll see the mouthprint on the belly where the eel has tapped her. Forget using any other bait up there. All those eels want is herring roe."

Across the road is a field full of big stumps, what's left after a big piece of land has been logged. In this part of the world, it seems like there are as many fields of stumps and undergrowth, looking like wounds in the woods-line, as there are fields of cotton or soybeans. Weyerhauser Paper Company owns vast tracts of eastern North Carolina, where they grow loblolly pines to convert into paper. It's a fast-growing tree, and can be harvested every 25 years or so. In addition to the trees they grow on their own land, paper companies are always ready to pay for timber from land that is not theirs.

"Weyerhauser just came in and took out 500 acres of timber there across the road," said Koonce. "Those trees were probably 60 or 70 years old. They've been looking the same size to me since I was a baby. Weyerhauser owns North Carolina. There's no telling how many millions of acres of timber they own. At least they'll guarantee to replant, which is more than some others will do."

Timber companies paid good money when they bought a stand of timber, five- or even six-figure sums. Timber was a crop in eastern Carolina. Once a generation, Weyerhauser came to harvest the loblollies they had planted on someone's land, and they left behind a torn-up stretch of ground and a big check. The presence of the paper companies was ubiquitous as one drove the back roads. If you weren't stuck behind a logging truck with a dozen big pines stacked and tied down with cables on the long bed, you were passing stands of timber being harvested or huge, long, laid-open fields where there was nothing left but a sea of broken stumps and sticks jutting up amid the dark brown of the overturned black-loam soil, roots ripped out of the ground where the timber had been "harvested," hacked out, chopped down, where the ruts left in the ground by the big log truck tires filled up with muddy water when it rained.

Gary Koonce sold most of the eels he trapped to Martie Bouw, but he admitted to dealing with Martie Bouw's mysterious competition every so often. He would not, or could not, throw any more light on the identity of the Philadelphia-based eel buyer, declining to provide me with a telephone number or a name. "The onliest name I know for him is Cigar. I don't know where I've put that number. I've got it around somewheres. He pays better'n Martie, but he won't even come unless you've got 1,000 pounds, so I sell most of mine to Martie. But, you're talking a 60-cent-a-pound difference between what Martie and Cigar pay, and if I have 2,000 pounds, that's $1,200 a load. You're gonna feel that."

After Martie brought a truckload of eels back to the concrete tanks beside his house, his next step was to grade them, so he would know how much of what size he had to offer his European customers. This was done using a metal contraption he had built about six feet off the ground outside the rear wall of the Holland Seafood plant. It was a slightly inclined chute, with four smaller chutes on its side that spewed eels, according to their sizes, into big, plastic tubs waiting below. These filled with eels classified as small, medium, large, and extra large. The small and medium-sized ones could be either males or females, but the large and extra large could only be females.

Males do not usually grow longer than about 18 inches, while the females grow twice as big, to around a yard long.

It was an impressive sight to stand over those tubs and look down into them, particularly the one that was full of extra large eels, fully grown females as long as an arm and as thick as a wrist. Their heads flared out from their backs in the arrowhead shape of a poisonous snake, and they were the size of full-grown, yard-long water moccasins. Their bodies rose and fell in a heaving, writhing mass, now and then a head rising up above the squirming knot in the tub—perhaps the startlingly blue eyes of a silver eel—and then sinking out of sight again below it. They moved with an equal fluidity backward and forward. An eel uses its tail like a hand to feel its surroundings, and with their tails they search to find an opening through which to escape. One managed to breach the tub, God knows how, winding up on the ground beside it.

"Pick it up," Martie told me, flicking his eyes in the direction of the escaped eel, already quickly squirming away across the wet concrete. I bent over and tried. And tried. And tried. For a moment I had my hands around the eel; then she would be gone, and I would be left with a handful of slime. Martie reached down to show me how to grasp an eel with a three-fingered grip, doing it exactly the way it was described in 1866 in an anonymously authored book called *Athletic Sports for Boys: A Repository of Graceful Recreations for Youth,* which included instructions for eel fishing: "Place the second finger on one side of him, and the first and third on the other, about an inch and a half from his neck. Then by pressing the fingers together he cannot move."

While Martie worked with the eels, Marie worked in the trailer beside their house that served as an office. Her tools were phone and fax as she lined up the people along the East Coast who had eels to sell to Martie and the people in Europe who wanted to buy them. Martie was always busy. If he was not out on the road hauling something behind the Volvo, there was surely something that needed doing at the plant. He worked six days a week, and had Marie not been firm in her insistence that no business be done on Sunday, he would have worked then, too.

Saturday afternoons, for instance, Martie often spent in the shed next to the plant, with a plastic tub full of dead eels, those that had not survived their capture and trip to Arapahoe in the live-haul truck. Some eels, though nothing is wrong with them, are killed by the stress of being trapped and transported. These he dressed out to be shipped to Holland or Germany for smoking. There is no perceptible difference in the flavor of eels that were killed just before being smoked and those that were killed, frozen, and then smoked. Traditionally, people liked to keep them alive until they were ready for the smoker, but customers would settle for less, and Martie could move a certain amount of frozen product, so he cleaned the dead ones and froze them until he had enough for a shipment. What the northern Europeans like best are the bigger, female eels, because the eel with the most fat is the tastiest when smoked. Many of the eels Martie was cleaning had been trapped on their way downriver, hunting one of the last meals they would ever think about eating. They were turning into silver eels, preparing for the long saltwater trip back to the Sargasso, females a yard long, eyes blue and opaque, bellies white.

Martie's two young blond, blue-eyed sons often joined him in his Saturday afternoon work. The youngest, six years old, lined the eels up on the aluminum cleaning table for his father to clean. Martie took an eel, stabbing a short-handled Phillips screwdriver behind its head and through a hole drilled in the table. Even a dead eel is a slippery creature, and this immobilized her. Then he slit the eel lengthwise down her long belly and scooped out the guts, which he tossed through a hole in the table to a box underneath for later disposal. When he slit open silver eels, they had a wall of fat running along the insides of their body cavities, a reserve of energy that they were building up in preparation for never eating again and for their last, long, deep swim. It is a piece of long-held eel lore that an eel's anal opening seals tightly shut when she reaches salt water on that homeward journey to the Sargasso, but it has not been proven experimentally.

"I learned how to gut an eel from a guy in Holland, and this was his job, every day," Martie told me, as he cleaned eels. "He worked at a plant, and his job was to gut eels all day long. Guys that do that in Holland have a long, specially manicured thumbnail to help them scoop out the innards. You can tell eel gutters by their thumbnails."

A little blood splashed up ahead of his broad, scooping thumb. "Umph, I got some in my eye," he muttered, and immediately set the eel down on the table and went over to a sink on the wall that had an arching, long-neck faucet, operated by a button a person could push with a knee, while standing bent under it. He bathed his eye.

"Eel blood and eel slime is toxic," he said, getting back to work at the table. "I ought to wear goggles, but I can't see so well with them. If you get eel blood in your eye and don't wash it out right away, you spend the whole day with everything hazy."

As Martie Bouw ran his fingers along the bellies of the silver eels before he opened them, he could tell how much fat there would be inside, what stage of development the eel's reproductive system had reached. "These are not things you can learn how to do in a book. I've been handling eels for 20 years. All I ask is that my boys don't do this. They can do whatever they like when they grow up, as long as it's not dealing eels. Why not? Take right now, for instance: there's a glut on the market; the superstrong dollar is killing me; the competition is trying to drive me out of business; the eelers all want to be paid the second I buy their eels; and an old customer just screwed me out of $60,000 by claiming 30 percent of his shipment arrived dead.

"No, I don't want these boys to grow up and be eel dealers."

CHAPTER 3
Guipúzcoa, Basque Country, Spain

A declining eel population is not a trend confined to the American side of the Atlantic. European catch numbers are way down as well, and by late 1999 the European Union had taken note of the problem, recommending the same course of action followed by North Carolina: ban elver fishing. A regulation was issued that would prevent exportation of elvers by the EU's 15 member countries. However, to take effect, it had to be signed off on by the ministries that control fishing in each of the member countries. Not much of a problem was expected in England, Denmark, or Germany because they had already banned elver fishing. Opposition was expected, though, in Spain and France, which had substantial elver fisheries and lots of sales to China.

The idea of banning elver fishing did not sit well at all, for instance, in the Basque region of northern Spain, particularly in the small town of Aguinaga, in the province of Guipúzcoa (*ghee-poos-qua*). The world of eels has a number of capital cities, and most of them seem to be towns with less than a thousand inhabitants. Aguinaga (*ah-ghee-nah-gah*), one of eeldom's most important centers with regard to elvers, is a town of 600.

The 15 miles of two-lane asphalt from the city of San Sebastián on Spain's northern coast inland to Aguinaga runs beside the rushing Oria River, along a gorge at the bottom of plunging green hillsides dotted with rocky outcrops and sheep grazing on the steep slopes. Whitewashed stone houses are perched in clearings among the pines. They are big, square, solid houses with red-tiled roofs. Guipúzcoa is a hilly fastness, where rivers tumble toward the Cantabrian Sea in the Bay of Biscay, a huge stretch of the Atlantic Ocean above northern Spain. The people who live here are self-sustaining and insular, different in physique, temperament, customs, and language from people in the rest of Spain. A Basque man is likely to be bigger and stronger than his counterparts elsewhere in the country. Basque sports typically consist of things like two men standing on logs and chopping away at them between their spread feet to see who could get through his first, or two competitors trying to lift the heaviest boulders. The language, Euskera, is thought to be one of the world's oldest. It is unrelated to any other Indo-European language. It predates Spanish by, perhaps, thousands of years, and the Basques are believed to be among Europe's most ancient ethnic groups.

The vertiginous green hillsides have been cultivated for millennia by small farmers and grazed by shepherds' flocks. Access to the sea has created generation after generation of fishing families along the coast, and some scholars believe the Basques beat Columbus to the New World by centuries, with fishing enclaves established to catch the tremendous numbers of cod off the coasts of New England and Canada. A driver heading north from the dry, brown province of Aragon enters Basque country through the gently undulating green and fertile lands of Navarra, southernmost of Spain's four Basque provinces. Then, continuing northward out of Navarra and into the province of Guipúzcoa, the hills rise up, becoming steep, green declivities, isolating their inhabitants from all that lies to the south, enclosing them in a world of steep-sided valleys with outlets at the sea. It was in the direction of these outlets that many Guipúzcoans traditionally turned when they had to leave home to earn a living.

Just downriver from Aguinaga, the Oria River flows into the Cantabrian Sea at the town of Orio. Here, bobbing at anchor by the public wharf, are two dozen brightly painted, 80-foot-long wooden anchovy boats. They make a picturesque sight for someone passing through, but for those who go out on the boats to net anchovies, from March to September, and then to longline for tuna until November, it is hard, risky work, during which they spend months at sea fishing, with only one day every couple of weeks to put into Orio, unload the catch, go home, see the wife and kids, do laundry, and go back to the boat.

From November to March the big boats are at anchor in Orio, and their crews have traditionally had little more to do than draw unemployment and fish for *angulas* (*ang-oo-las*), as elvers are called in Spanish. Even though this involved going out on the river during cold, rainy nights to dip and hoist nets, it was easy work compared to spending weeks away from home on the high sea and was much appreciated by the people who lived along the river's banks, all the more so because it was a business transacted in cash.

It was not every night of the season that there were *angulas*—called *txitxardin beltz* (black worms) in the Basque language—to be caught. Only when the tide was rising into the river after dark, when there was a new or full moon, did it bring huge numbers of elvers riding it, entering the fresh water to commence their lives as eels. They rode the tide in, close to the surface, a supple wall of tiny glass eels; then they went to the bottom to avoid being carried back out by the ebb tide. If there was a high rising tide and a full moon, the fishing would be best when there was also heavy cloud cover. Elvers liked to move in the dark, the darker the better, although as they became accustomed to fresh water this changed, and they sometimes traveled upriver in daylight.

Elvers were not the only thing that came in on a rising tide. "Used tampons and condoms and every other damned thing comes up in the nets with the *angulas*," said Juan Antonio Larrañaga, one February night as we talked on the wharf at Orio. The tide was, indeed, rising, as could be seen by the quantity of plastic bags and debris moving upriver past the wharf at a brisk clip. Larrañaga had been supplementing his income for years as an elver fisherman, an *anguleró*. "The elvers don't seem to mind all the trash. This is the best year for them that I can ever remember. We should get a bunch out there tonight."

The man on whose boat he fished, Ramon Uranga, also owned a tavern in Orio, and he did not go out elver fishing on high-tide nights until the last customer had gone home and his restaurant could be closed. I waited for him on the wharf with Juan Antonio Larrañaga one cold, rainy, full-moon night in February. The two men fished for elvers any night there was a strong tide coming into the Oria, and this was one that qualified. Numerous skiffs were already out, and we could see them moving up and down the river.

When Uranga showed up, he was wearing oilskins and had brought a pair for me. Uh-oh, I thought, looks like I'm going to pay for my trip with some hard work. Ungenerous and unworthy worries. He and Juan Antonio parked me up in the boat's bow with a bottle of beer as we trolled slowly up and down the river. Each man stood beside a large net with an eight-foot-wide bag made of fine-meshed cotton at the end of a long pole, which was mounted in a clamp on the side of the skiff that held it vertically in the water. Every few minutes, Ramon put the 12-foot skiff's inboard, two-stroke engine in neutral and engaged a motorized winch that hauled in some ropes attached to the nets, which the two men guided aboard and tipped out onto a piece of screen laid across a box. The trash stayed on top of the screen, and the elvers fell through to the box beneath. The net came in dripping water, but thanks to the winches it was easy to bring in; the work was wet, but not particularly strenuous.

"It's a little damp and cold sometimes, but it sure beats being out at sea for weeks at time like I've been doing every year for the past 17 years," said Larrañaga. "I'd do this every night of the year if I could, and never go back to sea. It's dangerous out there. I've had friends who died at sea. You hardly see your family. It's no life for a man, but what else can you do? Fishing for *angulas* is easy, and if it's a good season like this one has been, a man can make some decent money. In December, we caught 106 kilos [about 234 pounds]. They say this has been the best year ever."

Around Christmas, the price being paid to the *anguleros* by Aguinaga's five elver dealers was up around $120 a pound, and there were plenty of people willing to get a little wet and cold of an evening for that kind of money. Even in February, with the price down to $75 a pound, there were men lined up along the river's shore with slightly reduced versions of the same net used aboard the boats, dipping for the *angulas* that swam close to the bank. *Angulas* like to swim upriver where they encounter the least current, and this often turns out to be as close to shore as they can get. Each bank fisherman had a gas lantern on the ground at his feet, by the light of which he inspected his net each time he raised it out of the dark river flowing past him. Men in small pockets of lantern light lined the riverbank, raising and lowering their nets.

The Oria River has been through a number of phases in its ability to support an elver fishery. The *angulas* were so plentiful in the late 1800s that people stood on the bank scooping them out in makeshift nets and then using them to feed the pigs. In the mid-twentieth century, a paper mill was constructed not too far above Aguinaga, and the effluent from the mill reduced to practically nil the number of *angulas* that made it upriver even as far as the town. Then, the paper mill closed down and the elver fishing picked back up, although during the last half of the 1990s the fishery went into another precipitous decline. No one knew why, but the elvers stopped coming. Conservationists blamed it on a general degradation of water quality and habitat and saw it as the beginning of the end for elvers in Basque rivers. Their gloomy predictions seemed to be fulfilled in 1998, one of the worst elver seasons on record. Then, for no apparent reason, the 1999 season was what many were calling the best ever, with tremendous numbers of *angulas* coming into the Oria.

"It has been a good year, an amazingly good year," said Andres Bruño, 71, whose family has been buying and selling *angulas* in Aguinaga for three generations. "It just shows you that if you leave them alone they'll do fine. There's no need to regulate the elver fishery. I went to Brussels and told them that. No matter how good a year we have, and the same is true in France for the Loire, we don't catch more than 5 percent of them. Ninety-five percent of the elvers are not netted.

"What they need to be doing is regulating people in those countries where they fish for the females coming downriver, when they're going back to the sea. That's when they catch the females on their way to reproduce, each ready to produce up to 10 million eggs. That's what I told them in Brussels. They need to ban fishing for adults and there would be plenty of eels."

Like eelers in North Carolina, the Basque *anguleros* are perfectly content to practice their trade with a minimum of regulation from government authorities. Basques are notoriously independent-minded. They originally inhabited land on both sides of what is now the French-Spanish border. There are currently four Basque provinces within Spain, and three more above the border in France. While people of Basque origin in southern France are reasonably well integrated into French society, the same cannot, necessarily, be said for those in Spain. As the new millennium began, with Northern Ireland free of sectarian violence under a tenuous truce, the Basque separatist movement, ETA (the initials stand for *Euskadi Ta Askatasuna*—Euskadi and Freedom, *Euskadi* being the Basques' name for their country), had the dubious distinction of being the only group still carrying on a large-scale armed nationalist struggle in western Europe.

Aguinaga is a small town, with the smallest of public squares. Every exterior wall there is covered with ETA signage, as are most of the public walls all over Guipúzcoa. Big, black, angry letters, shouting slogans from the whitewashed walls. Whether they are ETA sympathizers or not, Basques have a reputation for being people who keep to themselves, mind their own business, and ask only to be left alone. They are inherently suspicious of Madrid, the European Union, and all other governments and peoples outside their hilly redoubt. While the majority of them are, no doubt, tired of ETA—tired of the terrorist violence and the "revolutionary tax" imposed on businesses to pay for it—they are also resentful of the endless police presence in their region and of the heavy-handed attempts by the federal government in Madrid to control them.

It is one another whom they trust. When I visited the tiny precincts of Aguinaga, teenagers were spending their weekends refurbishing a long, low building that had been provided for them by City Hall. They planned to use it as a meeting place in which to hold dances and lectures, someplace the town's young people could hang out. A youth center. The outside of the building was covered with ETA slogans which they were making no effort to cover over, and perhaps had put there themselves, but inside a group of a dozen teenagers were working hard, painting and cleaning, mopping the floors.

The Basque spirit has flowered in some surprising ways, far more innovative and peaceful than ETA's armed nationalism, and none more remarkable than the cooperatives of Mondragon, a factory town of 30,000 inhabitants. The town is deep in the heart of Guipúzcoa, by the Deba River, nestled in a narrow, verdant valley an hour or so inland from San Sebastián, surrounded by the low peaks of the Cantabrian Mountains—the tops of which are often wreathed in gray clouds, drifting like smoke through the branches of the dark green pines on the steep hillsides. The town has long been known for its industry, particularly its steel, and was renowned during the Middle Ages for its swords. Currently, the Mondragon Cooperative Corporation represents over 100 businesses and industries.

Amazingly, the cooperatives were begun by a modest, soft-spoken priest only two years after the end of the terrible Spanish Civil War, which lasted from 1936 to 1939, and in which more than a million Spaniards died. Nowhere was the war more bitterly fought than in Basque country, and when the rebel general, Francisco Franco, finally won, he banned everything connected to the region's ancient culture: language, dances, and festivals, as well as any nationalist political activity. All over Spain, during the 36 years of dictatorship that followed the war, communists were the putative enemy, and anything that had the faintest whiff of collective thinking was brutally repressed. Nowhere was this more so than in Basque country, so it was all the more remarkable that a lone priest could begin a movement in which workers owned the businesses where they labored.

Just two years after the war's end, on February 5, 1941, the Vitoria-Bilbao train discharged a single passenger at the Mondragon station. The tall man who alighted from the train that morning, José María Arizmendiarrieta, was a young, thin, myopic priest coming from seminary studies to take up his first parish assignment. Conditions were hardly promising. Mondragon had suffered heavily during the war, and at 26 years old, Father Arizmendiarrieta knew all about that suffering in his own flesh and bone.

Born in the small Basque town of Markina in 1915, Arizmendiarrieta committed to his religious vocation early. The oldest of four brothers, at the age of 12 he formally renounced the inheritance due him by virtue of his status as first-born. He was already prepared to devote himself to a life of Christian service. He went on to study philosophy at the seminary during the brief years of the left-leaning Spanish Republic. Franco's military uprising, in 1936, began while Arizmendiarrieta was home on summer vacation, and he joined the Republican Army, serving as a journalist. He and a friend founded, and reported for, two Republican newspapers. When Bilbao fell to the fascists in June 1937, they were arrested. His friend was executed by a firing squad, but Arizmendiarrieta was released on a technicality, with the stipulation that he had to serve in Franco's army until the war ended. After the war he returned to Vitoria to resume his seminary studies.

He officiated at his first Mass in his hometown of Markina on January 1, 1941, and was preparing to return to his university studies when he was assigned to Mondragon. He stepped off the train on a rainy, cold morning, apt weather for his arrival. Mondragon's 8,000 residents were in the midst of hard times that matched the winter climate. They were exhausted, wounded in spirit, and faced with material shortages on all sides. Unemployment was high, bread was rationed, and other food was scarce. The town's primary employer was a small iron foundry with a limited number of jobs.

The priest had read widely in philosophy, economic theory, and social relations during his years in seminary, and he was convinced that human beings could build a better world through their daily work. He also believed that it was his responsibility as a servant of God to help make this possible. Arizmendiarrieta found fertile ground for his ideas about how people should relate economically. He was searching for a third way between capitalism and communism, and Mondragon proved an excellent laboratory for developing it.

"The economic revolution will be moral or it will not be. The moral revolution will be economic or it will not be," Arizmendiarrieta wrote. He began his revolution with a polytechnic school for 20 students from Mondragon, which he financed by a local lottery and inaugurated in October 1943. The school would have over a thousand students by the time he died, in 1976. This small original group of students formed a nucleus of people who helped carry out his ideas in Mondragon. In 1959, the Caja Laboral, the bank that would finance the cooperatives, was opened without ceremony. It had made over 150 start-up business loans by 2000, on which none of the borrowers has defaulted. The cooperatives had about 42,000 members by the year 2000, and they had weathered Spain's deep recession in the early 1990s to enjoy strong years in the last part of the decade.

All of this began in a period, the early years of the Franco dictatorship, in which innovation was not encouraged in Spain, especially not in Basque country, where all deviations from the state/ church norm were viewed as potentially subversive. And it was all begun by one mild-mannered priest with a weak heart, whose most drastic bow to physical comfort came when he was 50 years old and agreed to accept the gift of a bicycle from his parishioners who were worried about his failing health and insisted that he stop walking everywhere he went.

The cooperatives have made a big difference in the Basque country economy, but there are still plenty of people whose wages fall far short of enough. In a good elver year, like the 1999–2000 season, lots of them become *anguleros,* and Chinese eel farms were standing by to purchase all they could. Eel farming in China means growing juveniles into adults to be killed, smoked, and processed in the way that Japanese consumers like them best: as *kabayaki.* This is a process in which chunks of eel are skewered, dipped in a sauce, and grilled. *Kabayaki* can be vacuum-packed and exported, and it is the way in which eels are served on sushi and sashimi. While the Chinese consume a lot of eel domestically, the majority of Chinese farms raise them for sale in Japan, where great quantities of *kabayaki* are consumed annually, with the lion's share coming from China. The Chinese prefer to use *japonica* elvers to grow the eels they will convert into *kabayaki,* but there are not nearly enough of them, so they import elvers from Europe and the United States and are willing to pay for as many as they can get. In 2000, elver dealers in Aguinaga were sending record numbers to China.

Aguinaga's *angula* dealers also serve a domestic market. People throughout northern Spain consider elvers a culinary delicacy. Christmas Eve is the traditional time to eat them, and even though prices can reach $250 a pound in the markets, people tend to splurge, at least once a year, and pay $120 at the market for a half pound, enough for two bowls' worth of what look like nothing so much as hair-thin, transparent worms. The Christmas season is the highlight of any year's elver fishing in Aguinaga. Whether there are lots of elvers being caught or only a few, this is when demand and prices will be at their peak, and year after year the price of *angulas* continues to rise. The phenomenon would be the envy of any marketing director, and no one can quite explain how it happens. What is certain is that the price of *angulas* has climbed by leaps and bounds since the 1960s, outstripping inflation, but Spaniards continue to buy them.

Still, elvers are not widely consumed, not even in all the countries that have a taste for adult eels. And while there are archaeological indications that eels may have been among the earliest fish eaten in Europe—remains of eels have been unearthed at Celtic ruins in Glastonbury, England, and at archaeological sites dating to the Paleolithic Age in France—there are no such signs pointing to elver consumption. Of course, since they are eaten whole, there is no sign left behind. Written reports are scant. It is known that within the last few centuries elvers have been eaten around the Severn River in England, the Loire in France, and Lake Comacchio in Italy, as well as in the north of Spain. Early mention is made of them by an Italian, Francesco Redi, who wrote that in 1667 nearly 3,000 pounds of elvers were taken from the Arno River in Pisa, where there is still a great fondness for them—particularly cooked in a light tomato sauce with grated parmesan cheese on top.

The English word "elver" is held by some to come from "eel-fare," the verb "to fare," "to travel" (as in "thoroughfare"), referring to the great highway of tiny eels entering rivers, or possibly from "eel-fair," referring to the celebrations held when the elvers migrated into rivers and were captured and eaten in great numbers. In 1748, Daniel Defoe, in his four-volume travel book, *Tour of Great Britain,* wrote of them being made into small cakes: "These elver-cakes they dispose of at Bath and Bristol."

As recently as 1978, Christopher Moriarty wrote in his book *Eels: A Natural and Unnatural History* that there were 90 regular elver fishermen on the Severn River, where people liked to fry them with a little bacon. An Englishman named Peter Dowdeswell, who was interviewed in a *New Yorker* magazine article in 1986, held the world record for elver eating, having devoured a pound of them in 13.7 seconds. He warned the magazine's readers: "It's not advisable for anyone to do what I do."

In Aguinaga, no one is certain just who was the first to stop throwing the *angulas* to the pigs and begin tossing them in a frying pan instead. The first dishes were mostly made with eggs—elvers in omelettes or mixed in with scrambled eggs. Then, someone hit upon *angulas á la Vizcaina,* elvers done Bilbao-style, and little by little that became about the only way you could find them prepared. *Angulas á la Vizcaina* are elvers flash-fried in cold-pressed, extra virgin olive oil and served in an earthenware bowl, with minced garlic and a pepper with a mild sting called a *guindilla.* They are served while still sizzling hot and are eaten with a wooden fork, because a metal utensil might burn the diner's lips. On the menus of San Sebastián's restaurants the price for them can reach $70–80 during the season for a serving of a quarter pound. They are quite tasty, like a slightly grainy pasta with a tiny crunch from the backbone and a faint aftertaste of fish and garlic, along with the *guindilla*'s light bite.

"It was a group of our grandfathers from Aguinaga that first began to eat elvers, and it was my father who began to sell them to restaurants here and began the first business with elvers," Santiago Otamendi told me. He was the sales director of El Angulero de Aguinaga, the business his grandfather had founded, one of five family-owned *angula* dealerships in the little village. "My father went down south of Tarragona to the Ebro delta, and in one night there they caught 1,100 pounds of elvers. There wasn't anyone doing it. He had to carry his net with him on the train from Aguinaga to Tarragona."

Gone now. In less than a century those walls of glass eels have been reduced to virtually nothing. There are still some eels in the Ebro River, but their numbers are greatly reduced, with elver recruitment practically nil, and in the Albufera, development and the runoff from rice fields has converted a beautiful estuary into a muddy, toxic lake, where eelers have seen eels all but disappear. They have been replaced in the local economy by rapidly growing numbers of the Louisiana red swamp crawfish, *Procambrus clarkii,* descended from a colony carried to Spain by James Avault, a professor of agriculture at Louisiana State University. The Louisiana crawfish, another animal that thrives in the mud, has even less need of relatively clean water than do eels, and it has kept something in the pots of former eelers in the Albufera, because there is a small market for the crawfish around Valencia and Barcelona. The occasional eel is still pulled out of the Albufera, but it is clear that the decline in water quality has made it a much less desirable place for them to spend any time, as either elvers or adults.

In Aguinaga, the elvers of the Oria River that escape the nets of the *anguleros* presumably make their way upriver to live out a long term as adults before heading back toward the Sargasso. The Basques do not eat or fish for eels once they have grown out of the *angula* stage, nor are more mature eels eaten in Asturias or Galicia, where elvers also enter the rivers and the local diet. Adult eels are eaten in Tarragona and Valencia, around the Albufera, but even in these parts of Spain they have not always been appreciated.

In fact, the Romans, who founded the city of Tarraco, later called Tarragona, around 200 B.C., held the freshwater eel in contempt, disdaining to eat it, although the eel's big, exclusively saltwater cousin, the conger, was highly esteemed. No one is sure why the Romans formed a distaste for the meat of freshwater eels. William Radcliffe speculated in his 1921 book, *Fishing from the Earliest Times,* that perhaps eels were unpalatable to the Romans because dried eel skins were twisted tightly together and worn as a kind of belt that was also used to give disciplinary lashes to unruly school boys. (Incidentally, the same use of eel skin was still being made in seventeenth-century England, when Samuel Pepys's diary entry for April 24, 1663, states: "With my salt eele, went down in the parler, and there got my boy and did beat him.")

Others attribute the Roman disinclination to eat them to the fact that eels were often to be found gathered around sewer outflows, making themselves perfectly at home in highly unsavory waters. The Roman satirist Juvenal heaps scorn on the head of a host who serves a guest an eel:

Now comes the dish for thy repast decreed,
A snake-like eel, of that unwholesome breed
Which fattens where Cloaca's torrents pour,
And sports in Tiber's flood, his native shore;

Or midst the drains that in Suburra flow,
Swims the foul streams, which fill the crypts below.

The eels that populated the rivers of pre-Christian Spain may not have gone entirely unappreciated, however, for the Greeks had a colony some hundred miles north of Tarragona in an area called Ampurdan, and Greek regard for freshwater eels was legendary. Fear death, wrote the Greek comic poet Philetaerus, who lived around the beginning of the fourth century B.C., "for when you're dead, you cannot then eat eels."

The best eels in the ancient world were said to come from Lake Copaïs in Boeotia, located northwest of Athens. The lake was drained by artificial canals many centuries ago, but in classical Greece it covered a large expanse of territory in the northern basin of Boeotia, fed by the Cephisus River. The Boeotians were often contrasted in Greek comedies with the Athenians, who considered themselves to be refined and reasonable, as opposed to the uneducated, greedy, brutish people of Boeotia. Nevertheless, one thing Athenians were willing to pay the Boeotians for, and pay dearly at that, was the eels from Lake Copaïs. Indeed, after wishing that Boeotia and all its inhabitants be destroyed, the title heroine in Aristophanes' *Lysistrata* added, "except the eels".

Even the Greeks did not treat the eel with as much respect as the Egyptians, who considered it a minor god. Herodotus, around the middle of the fifth century B.C., recorded that it was sacred to the Nile. Eels had their own cult following in Egypt, according to *Three Musketeers* author and chronicler of French eating habits Alexandre Dumas, in his *Grand Dictionnaire de Cuisine,* and were kept in ponds where they were fed daily, by a devotee, on cheese and the entrails of animals.

The Greek comic playwright Antiphanes, who wrote around 350 B.C., points out that the Greeks, in their way, paid more tribute to the eel than those who worshipped it: "They say that the Egyptians are clever in that they rank the Eel equal to a god, but in reality here it is held in esteem and value far higher than the gods, for *them* we can propitiate with a prayer or two, while to get even a smell of an Eel at Athens we have to spend twelve *drachmae* or more!"

Even more than we do today, the Greeks viewed the sea as a foreign element. Wealthy Greeks were willing to spend money to eat fish and seafood, providing a steady market for those who brought them to market, but to *be* a fisherman was a sign of abject poverty. It implied an absence of recourse that forced one to leave the earth to look for sustenance in the dangerous deeps, to live poorly and miserably in a hut by the sea. Foreign and threatening as the sea was, so too were its inhabitants. Fish were considered implacable foes of humans, ready to eat them should they have the misfortune to fall overboard.

"Lie there among the fish who will heedlessly lick the gore off your wound," Achilles curses the body of an enemy he has just thrown into the river in Homer's *Iliad,* written in the eighth century B.C. "Your mother won't mourn you laying on the bier . . . some fish will dart over, beneath the dark and rippling surface of the waves, and eat Lykaon's glistening fat."

Further along in the *Iliad,* Homer distinguishes the eel from all other fish, writing of them as two different things in a scene in which Achilles has vanquished Asterpaíos on the banks of a seagoing river:

> With this he pulled from the bank's overhang
> his bronze-shot spear, and having torn the life
> out of the body, left it there, to lie
> in sand, where the dark water lapped at it.
> Then eels and fish attended to the body,
> picking and nibbling kidney fat away.
>
> (trans. Robert Fitzgerald, 1974)

Eels are reputed to have saved the Greek colony of Syracuse, in Sicily, from becoming a battleground when the Carthaginian army arrived to conquer the city. Before facing each other to fight, Carthaginian and Syracusan soldiers went to hunt eels in the marshes around the city to make a prebattle repast, according to Waverly Root in his book *Food*. Once they had discovered their common bond of eel appreciation, they began to socialize and fraternize, and the Carthaginians decided to go home instead of fighting.

Eels certainly held a prominent place in ancient Greek cuisine, and while they were not worshipped, there are a few scattered references in Greek literature to the ritual killing of eels. Generally, however, the Greek regard for the fish was gastronomic rather than spiritual. Those who came as close as anyone to conferring sacred status on the pleasures of the table, in general, were the Sybarites, from the Greek community of Sybaris on Sicily, known for their extravagant excesses at the table and elsewhere. They were willing to pay for their pleasures, introducing economic incentives for cooks who invented new recipes and spending vast sums of money on banquets. Their respect for the culinary value of the eel was so high that they exempted eel sellers from all taxes in an effort to encourage the trade and keep the price down.

Although most Greeks did not confer sacred status on the eel away from the table, they recognized that it was a mysterious creature, markedly different from its fellow fish. Around the same time that Aristotle was compiling his *Natural History,* the Greek poet and parodist Mataro wrote of the eel lying in the embrace of the god Zeus. Rainwater came directly from Zeus, and it was widely believed that the reproduction of eels depended on rainwater.

Aristotle himself concluded:

Eels are not produced from sexual intercourse, nor are they oviparous, nor have they ever been detected with semen or ova, nor when dissected do they appear to possess either seminal or uterine viscera; and this is the only kind of sanguineous animal which does not originate either in sexual intercourse or in ova. It is, however, manifest that this is the case, for, after rain, they have been reproduced in some marshy ponds, from which all the water was drawn and the mud cleared out; but they are never produced in dry places nor in ponds that are always full, for they live upon and are nourished by rain water. It is plain, therefore, that they are not produced from either sexual intercourse or from ova. Some persons have thought that they were productive, because some eels have parasitical worms, and they thought that these became eels.

This however, is not the case, but they originate in what are called the entrails of the earth, which are found spontaneously in mud and moist earth. They have been observed making their escape from them, and others have been found in them when cut up and dissected. These originate both in the sea and in rivers wherein putrid matter is abundant: in those places in the sea which are full of fuci [seaweeds], and near the banks of rivers and ponds, for in these places the heat causes much putridity. This is the mode of generation in eels.

(trans. Richard Cresswell, 1862)

Most Greek scholars have translated Aristotle as asserting that eels are actually born from the mud. A few have held, however, that he was referring to larvae in the mud, not a spontaneous generation of eels from wet ground, which would be much closer to the current understanding of an eel's life cycle, which does begin with larvae. Regardless, the eel has been a problem for natural historians from Aristotle's day to the present. Its genitalia are practically invisible, even under patient scientific scrutiny, and its activities are generally unobservable.

Some traditional notions about eels have been downright strange. A common belief in the British Isles held that eels were produced when stallions drank at the edge of a river and the hair of their tails fell into the water. On the north coast of Germany, a fish related to the cod, *Zoarces viviparous,* which gives birth to live young, is called *Aalmutter,* eel mother, because it was believed to be the fish from which eels were born. In Sardinia, it was thought that eels were born from a particular kind of beetle.

The confusion over how eels reproduce was compounded by the

fact that the parasites occasionally seen inside adult eels were mistaken for fetal eels, so it was believed by many for a long time that eels were viviparous, that they gave birth to live young. Aristotle expressly denied this from the beginning, holding that the objects sighted were probably intestinal worms, and he was right, but it took a long time to prove it. The first respected scholar to insist on the eel's viviparity was the thirteenth-century naturalist and Dominican brother Albertus Magnus, in his *Book of Animals;* and Antonie van Leeuwenhoek in 1692 made the mistake of identifying the eel's bladder as its womb and declaring that the parasites found therein were elvers ready to be born. Carolus Linnaeus, the great giver of names and classifier of plants in the mid-1700s, also believed the eel was viviparous. The first to find ovaries in a female eel was Italian Carlo Mondini, who described the "frilled organs" in 1777, in his book *De Anguillae Ovariis.* Until then, the long ribbon of fan tissue along the walls of the eel's body cavity had been identified as adipose tissue. It took another hundred years to describe the male reproductive organs. Three years after Freud published his work identifying the looped organs of immature eel testes, the Polish naturalist Szymon Syrski definitively described a male eel's reproductive genitalia in 1880.

Once it had been established to scientific satisfaction that the eel reproduced like most fish—oviparously, by means of deposited, fertilized eggs—some felt that it would soon give up the rest of its secretive life to scientific scrutiny. It was not to happen, although another piece of the puzzle of the eel's life cycle, its metamorphosis, fell into place shortly thereafter. Eel larvae had been found and recorded by William Morris as early as 1763 in the Irish Sea near northern Wales, but they were not extensively described until 1856, when a German naturalist named Kaup wrote about them. He described a larva he had found in the Straits of Messina off Sicily, which he described as looking like a willow leaf and which he named *Leptocephalus brevirostris.* The name *Leptocephalus* is applied to a larva that looks like a leaf, and it is used to describe any such animal. It was not recognized that *brevirostris* was actually an immature eel until

1896, when two Italian naturalists reported that they had watched a leptocephalus turn into an eel in an aquarium at their laboratory in Messina. And, in 1902, a pair of Americans, Carl Eigenmann and Clarence Kennedy, described two specimens of American eel larvae that had been found in the Atlantic, off the New England coast, in 1883. Even then, it was assumed that the leptocephali were found in the general area where they had been spawned. For instance, the larvae found at Messina were believed to be the result of eels spawning deep in the Mediterranean. In 1903, a Danish research vessel, the *Thor,* was put to work in the service of a new multinational research program called the International Investigations of the Sea, and in 1904 a young oceanographer named Johannes Schmidt was hired to come aboard and organize the effort to find the eel's spawning ground. By the time he found it, he was no longer young.

He began by trawling the Mediterranean for two years, examining great quantities of larvae, but all the specimens he found were 60–84 millimeters (approximately 2.3–3.3 inches) long—older larvae. Schmidt realized that he would have to begin trawling for larvae in the Atlantic, looking for the quintessential needle in a haystack, searching for a larva less than a quarter of an inch long in the middle of the Atlantic Ocean. Even so, he could not have imagined it would take him 18 more years; but given the delays and interruptions occasioned by financial shortfalls and the First World War, it was not until 1924 that he announced to the world that he had found the tiny larvae for which he was searching. He had gone through four research vessels looking for them, including the beautiful *Dana 1,* a four-masted schooner. In the introduction to his landmark report to the Smithsonian Institution, Schmidt wrote of his work: "The task was found to grow in extent year by year, to a degree we had never dreamed of; in fact, we have been obliged, in order to procure the necessary survey material, to make cruises of investigation ranging from America to Egypt, from Iceland to the Cape Verde Islands. And this work has been handicapped by lack of suitable vessels and equipment and by shortage of funds."

The search for juvenile larvae was arduous. By December 1913,

Schmidt's Atlantic Ocean trawls had turned up a larva—one larva—as small as 17 millimeters (two-thirds of an inch), and that was enough to keep him going. This larva had been taken in the Sargasso, and Schmidt decided to concentrate his efforts there, but his ship, the *Margrethe,* ran aground on a West Indian island and was ruined. The First World War was beginning, and he could not get another ship of his own, so he enlisted Danish steamships that were crossing the Atlantic to gather specimens. His persistence began to pay off. By the summer of 1914, he had more than a dozen specimens under 25 millimeters (about an inch), including one as small as 9 millimeters, less than a half-inch. Shortly thereafter, the war completely halted collection efforts, but in 1920 he managed to get another research vessel for trawling, and in 1922, south of Bermuda and east of Florida, he found more of the tiny larvae. In an article published in the Smithsonian Institution's annual report for 1924, he was able to assert that the eel spawns in the spring in the Sargasso Sea, and he included his photographs of eel larvae in various stages of their metamorphosis from juvenile to adult leptocephali, which are still the best photographs ever published of the elver's transformation from larvae into eels.

There, in 1924, stood the sum of the world's knowledge of eel reproduction. And, essentially, there it stands today. While there has been a vast leap forward in the knowledge of what eel eggs and sperm are composed of, and how to affect them, eels still have never been observed mating, have never mated in captivity, and have never, as live eels returning to their mating grounds, been captured in the open ocean.

It is not for lack of trying. The greatest eel scientists of the twentieth century have mounted expeditions. In 1979, the renowned German eel biologist, Friedrich-Wilhelm Tesch, whose 443-page book *Der Aal* (*The Eel*) is the standard text on the animal, headed up the Sargasso Sea Expedition, organized by the International Council for the Exploration of the Sea and the European Inland Fishery Advisory Committee. No live adults were captured, though many leptocephali were captured in trawls. Four silver eels were treated with pituitary extracts to bring them to sexual ripeness, then released into the Sargasso and tracked. They swam at anywhere from 700 yards deep to just below the surface, heading toward what Tesch called the "central spawning area" of the sea. Their signals were lost, however, before much data could be obtained. In 1993, another German expedition, aboard the research vessel *Poseidon* came back from the Sargasso with equally inconclusive results.

On the American side of the Atlantic, the eminent eel researcher James McCleave, professor and associate director at the University of Maine's School of Marine Sciences, oversaw a Sargasso expedition in 1989 on board a boat equipped with extremely sensitive sonar equipment. The idea was to locate groups of living animals in the Sargasso at what should be the right depths and temperatures for eels, then trawl with nets in search of adults. There were lots of sonar "sightings" that the research crew was certain represented eels, but not a single adult was netted.

"I think trying to catch them at sea is problematic," McCleave told me. "Maybe we were being a bit naive. Perhaps the best thing to do, if you had an unlimited amount of money, would be to develop transmitters that were small enough so you could put them on fish and they'd communicate to your ship or a satellite, so you could track them and find out how deep they swim, what routes they use, and how long it takes to reach their spawning grounds."

McCleave has been at the University of Maine since 1968, but he grew up in the Midwest, and he still has the accent to prove it. Even up here in the middle of Maine his lecturer's voice has the flat, unexcited tones of Kansas and Illinois, not the deep and singing downeasterner's accent. Lean and middle-aged, with thinning blond hair and gold-rimmed glasses, he was wearing a T-shirt, shorts, and gym shoes on the August day when I went to see him at his office. The campus was as deserted as a seaside town in winter; there was not a student in sight. The first thing a visitor to the University of Maine sees is a long row of fraternity houses at the front of the campus. In summer, they were as empty and quiet as abandoned birds' nests.

"The routes eels use to reach their spawning grounds are still a mystery," McCleave told me. "I teamed up with a guy who's an expert in using acoustics to locate aggregations of fish. Our idea was that maybe we could locate spawning aggregations and put down a trawl and catch them.

"We did a lot of steaming and a lot of processing of acoustic data, and we found some places where we got targets that were of the right strength that they might have been eels. There are not many things the size of an eel in the Sargasso, but we were in a research vessel and not a big commercial fishing vessel, so by the time we'd get the ship turned around, the net in the water, and go back to an area, we'd never see the targets again. So the upshot is that we never caught anything."

One thing is certain: for eel larvae it is a long, dangerous trip from the Sargasso toward fresh water. A wide variety of fish and birds feed on leptocephali. The estimated three years it can take a larva to reach fresh water in Europe and begin to transform into an eel is longer than the life expectancy of many fish species. Maybe it is the hard journey and tremendous struggle that give elvers their flavor.

San Sebastián is the closest big city to Aguinaga, only ten miles to the north. It is a lovely city by the Cantabrian Sea, built primarily in the mid-1800s to be a summer watering hole for Spanish royalty. Since the Guggenheim Museum opened in Bilbao in 1997, that city has become the most visited, after Madrid and Barcelona, in Spain; but San Sebastián, about 60 miles to the east of Bilbao along the coast, is the most beautiful of the Basque cities. It is renowned for its cuisine and the devotion of its citizens to good food. A centuries-old tradition of male cooking clubs exists in this city, and there is a deep respect for the rites of the kitchen. To cook professionally in Basque country, and particularly in San Sebastián, is to work in the big leagues of European cuisine. To prepare exquisite dishes for a living there may be as competitive as anywhere else in the world. When the subject of *angulas* comes up, chefs get serious. Their way of cooking and serving *angulas* has become a benchmark dish for them. Always expensive, wholly Basque, there is a way to do it, and, uncomplicated as it is, it needs to be done correctly.

When Tiburcio Eskisabel Lukas cooks an order of *angulas,* he is at the top of his form. His restaurant, Tiburcio's, is one of many on a four-block stretch of a street named Fermín Calbetón in San Sebastián, and it is one of the best, begun by Tiburcio's grandfather, with whom he shares a first name. Tiburcio, a rounded, chef-sized man, brandished a bottle of olive oil: "Only the finest of olive oils, extra virgin and from the first cold pressing," he admonished, a round steel frying pan raised in his other hand. He swooped the pan down to land on one of the six burners of the industrial-size gas stove where he works in the kitchen behind his eight-table dining room. When the oil in the pan was hot, he added chopped garlic and a *guindilla* pepper. Spaniards, generally, do not like hot food and grow only a couple varieties of hot peppers. The *guindilla* is a long, red pepper, mildly hot, that looks something like a cayenne and is most often used dried or chopped. Tiburcio added the *angulas* and let them sizzle a moment. They are sent out to a diner in a small round clay bowl with the trademark wooden fork. In this case, he invited me to eat them, and I wasted no time in accepting his offer. It was February, and the quarter-pound serving of elvers would have fetched around $60. Tiburcio buys his *angulas* from Aguinaga, and around Christmas, when the price starts to reach $75 a serving, he buys only when he has an advance order. Too expensive to hold, he said. At other seasons, he usually keeps a few orders' worth on hand.

The astronomical level of *angula* prices is nothing new. Newspaper articles from 30 or 40 years ago report record high prices being asked for *angulas,* even then. One Basque company developed a process to make what look like *angulas* out of surimi, a paste made from trash fish. They named the product *gula,* and in 2000, a quarter-pound jar sold for about $4.00 in the supermarket. The substitutes look pretty much like *angulas,* but even $4.00 is too much to pay if you ask an *angula* fancier.

"They ought to pay you to eat those things," said Tiburcio. "When you chew *angulas* they disappear, they melt on your tongue;

but when you chew *gulas,* they are really more like having a wad of plastic in your mouth."

The *gula* industry may have the last laugh, though, if the European Union gets its way about banning elver fishing. Despite the assertion of Aguinaga's *angula* dealers that what needs to be banned is fishing for females on their way downriver to the sea, it will take a lot more good years with high numbers of elvers appearing in Europe's rivers to discourage efforts to prohibit *angula* fishing.

The unequivocal recommendation of the EU's Scientific, Technical, and Economic Committee for Fisheries (STECF), issued in Brussels in November 1999, called for reducing elver fishing "to the lowest possible levels. . . . As a first step, STECF considers that countries should be encouraged to stop the direct consumption of glass eel and to ban the export of glass eel to countries outside the EU."

In the 1996–97 elver season, China imported about 150 tons of elvers from France, 30 tons from the United Kingdom, and 70 tons from Spain, for a total of 250 metric tons, or 550,000 pounds, of *Anguilla anguilla.* At 1,500 elvers to a pound, that's a big reduction in Europe's potential eel population. Apart from the depletion of Europe's stock, a serious problem in the export trade with China is the high mortality rate when the eels are shipped. The dealers in Aguinaga suffer mortality rates in transit that Martie Bouw, or almost all other fish dealers, would be absolutely unwilling to accept. It is estimated that in some shipments as many as 50 percent of the elvers shipped die en route. Another 20 percent are estimated to die in China before they can be harvested and sold as adults. The prices being paid the Chinese by the Japanese, who ultimately purchase most of the farmed eels, are, obviously, extremely high if the Chinese can still make money after losing up to 70 percent of the stock they buy.

By 1999, Portugal and Ireland had banned the export of elvers, and the following year all the EU members had signed off on the recommended prohibition, although the ban was still not in effect in early 2001. The legislation was not initially welcomed by Spain and France. Their opposition was tempered, however, by assurances that sales within Europe would be allowed under the legislation. This meant that elver dealers in Aguinaga and around the Loire River in France could still sell to Sweden or Holland, and the prohibition was expected to increase supply to European eel farmers and help develop local eel aquaculture by keeping the prices of elvers reasonable for eel growers. Sales to China would be banned, a measure that was seen as a necessary first step toward meaningful protection of the fish.

"We have to try and do something," said Ramon Franquesa, a marine economy expert from Barcelona who sat on the committee that recommended EU quotas for marine species. "We cannot just let the stocks be destroyed. Doing nothing would also destroy the industry. Look at cod—the disappearance of the resource destroyed hundreds of jobs and left banks with bad loans made to cod fishermen for expensive equipment."

CHAPTER 4

Lough Neagh, Northern Ireland

Concern about the decreasing numbers of elvers in Europe was nowhere greater than at the Lough Neagh (pronounced *lock nay*) Fishermen's Cooperative Society, in Toomebridge, Northern Ireland. The elvers that will grow into Lough Neagh eels come up the Bann River, from the Irish Sea, to the lake (lough) where they will spend their lives, and the year 2000 marked one of the worst years of elver recruitment on record there. Lough Neagh is the largest freshwater lake in the United Kingdom, and its eels are the most sought after adult eels in Europe. The director of the fishermen's cooperative, a 70-year-old priest named Oliver Kennedy, viewed the reduced numbers with alarm. The fishermen's society has gone so far as to buy elvers from dealers around England's Severn River in years when local elver recruitment was low, and the elvers cost a lot of money.

Kennedy maintained that the eels of Lough Neagh were the cooperative's most important asset, and he insisted on practicing conservation of the resource by keeping its numbers stable. To do so, he estimated that he needed to put some 4 million elvers a year in Lough Neagh, which he could do, in a year when a lot of elvers entered the Bann, wholly from the elver traps that the cooperative maintained at the river's mouth. To make the 26-mile journey upriver to the lake would take the elvers, on their own, about a year, so they were trapped when they entered the river from the Irish Sea, put in a live-haul tank mounted on the bed of a pickup, and trucked to the lake, in a trip that took about an hour. The traps captured most of the elvers entering the Bann, but, in the year 2000, numbers were down. Way down. Only about 1.5 million had been captured during the May–July elver season. Elvers cost about $150 a pound, and at 1,500 elvers to a pound, it meant the cooperative would have to spend about $250,000 to make up the shortfall. For Father Kennedy, doing what was necessary to conserve the lake's stocks was critically important, but with the eel business feeling the negative effects of a strong pound sterling—customers on the Continent were buying elsewhere so they could get more eels for their currency—he loathed the idea of spending the money.

"Most biologists are concerned by the fact that all other wild eel fisheries, except for ours, are in decline," he told me, as we sat in his office overlooking a weir that stretched almost all the way across the river, where each fall some 300,000 pounds of silver eels were trapped as they headed down the Bann from Lough Neagh toward salt water, on the first leg of their journey home to the Sargasso Sea.

Oliver Kennedy was a stout man, with a fringe of white hair and a ruddy face. He came to work at the cooperative without his clerical collar, but still dressed in black. He continued to fulfill his pastoral duties while working as one of Europe's most important wild eel dealers. "The eel stocks in other places have been overfished, and increasing numbers of younger eels are being caught," he told me. "Also, there is no effort being made to replenish stocks by bringing in elvers. Here in Lough Neagh we have controlled the annual catch, and in years when elver recruitment has been poor we have bought elvers from the Severn-Gloucester area of England."

The cooperative's members were Catholics, and many of them were militantly sympathetic to the Irish Republican Army (IRA). Some were, no doubt, members. "I'm not interested in the political side of it at all," said Kennedy. "My sole concern in organizing the fishermen's cooperative was in trying to see that people earn as good a living as is reasonably possible from what is, after all, one of the biggest natural assets in the province. It was unacceptable that the real profits of that fishery should, in the past, have been going to people who were effectively absentee landlords."

Another priest, another cooperative, another armed nationalist struggle. Northern Ireland, along with Basque country, was among the late twentieth century's European killing grounds, the places where nationalist groups were using armed terror to press their causes. The once-vast global British Empire was virtually reduced to these six counties in Ireland, one of Britain's earliest colonies and the last still struggling for independence. For centuries, the British took the best land for their own and promoted a vision of the Irish as second-class citizens: Catholic, uncivilized, uneducated, and unfit to govern themselves. What was passing in the year 2000 for a religious conflict between the Protestant descendants of the British colonists and the Catholic descendants of the native Irish was, in reality, more of a class struggle between those who had and those who had not, those to whom much had been given and those from whom much had been taken away. In the same way that elvers formed part of the economy that sustained ETA members in Basque country, so adult eels had long provided basic income to some of those who were left landless when the British Crown claimed the fertile farmland around Belfast for its "plantations" 400 years ago and left the indigenous Catholic population to wrest what it could from the rocky, wet ground around Lough Neagh.

The lake is some 16 miles long and 10 miles wide, one of the five largest in Europe. It is mostly surrounded by gently sloping green fields, grazed by cattle. To the east of the lake, visible from its waters on those days when it is not socked in by gray, are the Mourne Mountains. Lough Neagh is home to what most experts agree is the tastiest eel in all of Europe. It has a high fat content and a rich flavor that makes it prized above all others for smoking. The eelers attribute this to the eel's diet, which they say is particularly high in what is known as the Lough Neagh fly, an insect that looks like a gauzy-winged mayfly and belongs to the same family of insects. The Lough Neagh fly lays her eggs in a sac on the water; the sac sinks to the muddy bottom of the lake, and the larvae that hatch out provide a major source of sustenance for eels during their peak feeding seasons. Even so, many of the insect larvae escape being eaten to rise to the surface and fly. They do not bite, but during summer months they hover in irritating clouds around the head of any human in a still boat.

Whatever the reason, Lough Neagh eels are particularly tasty, and people have been eating them for at least 2,000 years, according to archaeological evidence in the area, where the remains of eel spears that old have been unearthed. In 1605, under pressure from the English Crown, the Gaelic-Irish earls who held the lease on the eel fishing rights in Lough Neagh gave it up as part of a trade-off for being allowed to abandon their properties to Protestant hands and flee into exile with their lives. The eel fishing rights were no small loss, as even then Lough Neagh had one of the most lucrative eel fisheries in Europe. The lease was for a period of 5,000 years, and the Protestants passed it down through a series of English lords and earls until, in 1661, it came to rest with the Earl of Shaftesbury's family.

Almost 300 years later, in 1959, the lease was allotted by the earl's family to a consortium owned by five men, known collectively in the eel industry of the time as the Ring. They were four London eel dealers and a Dutchman, and they had absolute control of the Lough Neagh fishery. They were primarily interested in silver eels, in letting the eels in the lake mature and capturing them in weirs when they came back downriver en route to the Sargasso. Local eelers who wanted to fish for yellow (or brown, as they call them in Ireland) eels in the lake had to buy a license from the company. There were company patrol boats, and eelers found working without company approval would have their gear seized. All eels caught under license had to be sold to the Ring, and the prices paid were set from London.

"The land within a half mile of the shore was left to Catholics, the people of my parish, when their forefathers were driven off the better, much more fertile land farther inland," Father Kennedy told me, leaning back in his chair behind his wide desk and gazing out the window to the weir on the Bann River below.

"Families were large and incomes were terribly small when I got here in 1961. There was never enough money to go around. I saw that I would have to learn about eels, and set about doing so. From the beginning it appeared to me to be a total anachronism that in the twentieth century one commercial enterprise could control a major inland fishery the size of Lough Neagh."

A group of eelers came to Oliver Kennedy in 1963, desperate and asking for help. He recommended that they form a trade union, and they did, calling it the Lough Neagh Fishermen's Cooperative Society. In 1965, one of the five Ring members put his 20 percent share up for sale, and two of the other directors, because they did not want a third to acquire it, offered the share to the fishermen's society. The eelers of Father Kennedy's parish subscribed $65,000 — another $60,000 was borrowed from a Belfast bank — and were given a share in the cooperative. Subsequently, under Oliver Kennedy's guidance, money was put aside each year for the eventual purchase of the remaining 80 percent interest in case it came up for sale. It was not too long before the remaining directors sold their shares, and, in 1971, the cooperative acquired the entire lease.

Members of the Ring later said that considerable pressure was brought to bear on them by militant Republican eelers, and during the years after the association acquired its 20 percent there had been a notable increase in people fishing without a license and selling to whomever they wished. The possibility for violent confrontation between the company's patrol boats and eelers was escalating, particularly taking into account that the latest round of the Troubles, the violence between Protestants and Catholics, had begun in 1968 and would not cease for 30 years.

"It was understood that if the eel fishermen didn't get the remaining shares of the lease that month in 1971, the next month there wouldn't have been anything to have a share in," according to one Londoner who was close to the negotiations. "Those fishermen up there are all IRA."

Regardless of the politics of those who do it, eel fishing in the lake is hard labor. The main method has always been handlining, setting out four long lines every day, some six miles' worth, each with 400 freshly baited hooks on it. Draft nets are allowed and occasionally used—they need to be set and pulled a couple dozen times a day—but the majority of the eels are still caught on handlines. The fresh bait is usually earthworms or what are called "poll," which are the minnows of a herring that was itself once the object of a big industry in the lake and now provides its young to the bait nets thrown by fishermen before they go out to set lines.

Most days of the year, the weather on the lake can be summed up as cold and wet. Even on rare, sunny days, there is little recreational use made of the lake. Lough Neagh is not a place for pleasure boats, but for men hauling a living out of its waters. The eelers work in pairs on fishing boats that are generally 26 feet long and powered by a six-cylinder inboard engine. The boats have a small covered space up front, but they feature mostly open deck on which to work. Both lines and nets are set aft, meaning the fishermen are exposed to whatever weather there is. About 200 boats make up the licensed fleet, and since each carries two men, Oliver Kennedy reckoned that some 400 families were dependent on the eel fishery. The eel season opens on May 1 and lasts until late autumn, when the water becomes cool enough to send the eels down into the mud, where they will hibernate until the water warms again.

"We fish from 4:00 A.M. Monday morning until noon on Saturday," Patrick Johnston told me one afternoon in the summer of 2000, as we sat on his boat. He was a big, ruddy-faced man, nearly 60 years old, who had been fishing for eels on the lake since he left school to do it with his father in 1957. "Saturday afternoon and Sundays are days of rest. Every other morning, we're out here at four in the morning to start pulling in lines. We'll meet the cooperative's live-haul truck with our catch; they'll take the eels back to the plant; and we'll take a break for a bit of breakfast, then get bait, and the cooperative allows us to start setting lines at 1:30 in the afternoon. When that's done, you can head in, but it's a long day."

He and his younger fishing partner, Jeff, sat in the stern on either side of a shallow wooden box that had a cord line coiled in it. Attached to this main line by thin, 18-inch pieces of nylon fishing line were the hooks, one for every few yards of cord. Every few hooks, a stone was attached to the line to hold it on the bottom. The nylon line used to be cotton twine, and the boats were powered by sails instead of engines, but otherwise the system was much the same as it has been for centuries.

The line uncoiled from the box between them, and they alternated taking its hooks, baiting them with a small, wriggly red earthworm from a box on each of their laps, which held a little soil and a lot of worms. The men tossed the line and baited hooks out the stern behind them as the boat moved slowly forward, controlled by Johnston with a pedal beside his foot. It took them a couple of hours each afternoon to lay out the lines, and another three to run them the next morning. They worked at a steady pace, baiting the hooks and paying out the line behind the boat. While they worked, they could chat, or watch each other, or look across the lake, and all the while their hands would keep baiting hooks and tossing them aft in one long, fluid motion. After so many years, they did not need to watch what they were doing; they worked by feel. They slid the worms on each hook as quickly and casually as someone putting on a sock and pulling it up. Eelers cultivated their own worms, and had their favorite places to dig for them, but it still took a couple of hours each day to dig up enough for the 1,600 hooks they would set.

"My father, and my father's father, fished for eels," Johnston told me. "They didn't swim a lick. In those days they used small boats with oars and sails. Eleven men died in one storm in the early 1900s, and men drowned fairly regularly in those years. These days, the biggest danger is that you'll slip on a wet deck and break an arm or a leg."

I

The lough will claim a victim every year.
It has virtue that hardens wood to stone.

There is a town sunk beneath its water.
It is the scar left by the Isle of Man.

II

At Toomebridge where it sluices towards the sea
They've set new gates and tanks against the flow.
From time to time they break the eels' journey
And lift five hundred stone in one go.

III

But up the shore in Antrim and Tyrone
There is a sense of fair play in the game.
The fishermen confront them one by one
And sail miles out, and never learn to swim.

IV

"We'll be the quicker going down," they say—
And when you argue there are no storms here.
That one hour floating's sure to land them safely—
"The lough will claim a victim every year."

(From "A Lough Neagh Sequence" [1969] by Seamus Heaney)

It is hard work fishing Lough Neagh, a bone-breaking damp cold to be borne through many a day, but Patrick Johnston was able to provide for his family better than his father or his grandfather had been able to provide for theirs. The cooperative allowed him a maximum daily catch of eight stone—112 pounds—of eels, and he was paid up around $2.00 a pound. It was a long day, but if a boat caught its maximum, each eeler made $100, and that, at least, constituted a living wage.

"When the cooperative was formed in 1965, the fishing community was depressed and basically deprived," Kennedy told me. "Ten and fifteen members to a family, all living in a small cramped house on the shore of the lough. It was essential to build up their self-confidence by getting them a reasonable standard of living.

"Now, their livelihoods have improved considerably. They're earning a much better living, and to their credit a high percentage of them have put their money to good use. They've bought themselves new homes, and a number of children from around the lough have gone on and gotten a higher education."

For more than two decades, the lion's share of Lough Neagh's eel production has gone to Holland, although in 1971, when the co-operative first acquired the lease, the vast majority of the eels were still being sold to London, just as they had been for centuries. Eels had always fed Londoners. Recipes for eel abound in the earliest cookbooks, and we know that in the smoky, wet streets of Dickensian London they were consumed in great quantities. They came to be particularly associated with the Cockneys who lived in London's East End, but eel consumption was not restricted to any one part of the city. A description of the animated state of things, in 1853, was penned by C. David Badham in his book *Prose Halieutics or Ancient and Modern Fish Tattle:*

London, from one end to the other, teems and steams with eels, alive and stewed; turn where you will, hot eels are everywhere smoking away, with many a fragrant condiment at hand to make what is in itself palatable yet more savoury; and this too at so low a rate, that for one halfpenny a man of the million may fill his stomach with six or seven long pieces, and wash them down with a cupful of the glutinous liquor in which they have been stewed. The traffic of this street luxury is so great that £20,000 sterling is annually cleared by it. 1,136,830 pounds' weight, on an average, are bought from Billingsgate [Market] every year by itinerant salesmen, who cook and retail them on their different beats: customers are not entirely confined to the lowest orders; some of the inferior "bourgeoisie" condescend to frequent the stands of the most noted retailers; and there are instances reported by some of those hawkers, of individuals coming twice a day for months and eating to the alarming extent of twopence at a time, or, in other words, of devouring from thirty to forty lengths of stewed eel, and decanting down their throats six or seven teacupfuls of the hot liquor.

Most of London's demographic changed drastically in the last quarter of the twentieth century, however, including that of the East End, with Cockney families moving out, many to the suburbs, leaving much of the area to a rising number of immigrants flowing into the neighborhood. The population of newcomers from places like Bangladesh and Turkey grew so much in the East End that by the year 2000, their cultures were far more important to the economic life of the local markets and stores than were Cockney tastes. Places serving carry-out curry or doner kebabs were on every street corner, but nowhere could you buy a cup of eels. Nor did the taste for *Anguilla* follow the Cockneys out to the suburbs. Somewhere it got lost in the assimilation process. In the suburbs it was far easier to find a place to eat a cheeseburger—for those who didn't know or worry about mad cow disease—than an order of stewed eels. In short, fewer and fewer Londoners were making their livelihoods from eel, and the city had fallen off the map of the world's eel capitals, where it had been for so long.

"It's a dying industry," Mick Jenrick told me, in his broad East End accent—and he ought to know. He was pretty much the king of what was left of the eel wholesalers. A short, pugnacious, barrel-shaped man with a nearly shaved head, he had a stall in the Billingsgate Market, the new one out by the waterside Docklands development in East London, and it was the only eel stall in the market. He had a plant close by, where he turned live eels into chunks of jellied ones, which he then sold wholesale by the dish—35 pieces of jellied eel packed into a round, plastic, Tupperware-like container.

Mick Jenrick had been in the eel business for 36 years when I talked to him in 2000. He began selling eels when he was 17. Eels were what he knew. His father had sold jellied eels from a stall at a nearby race track. His mother would clean them, cut them into chunks, and pour the liquid gelatin around them. Then she would pack a dish of them in ice, and they would jelly. Then and now, individual portions of jellied eels were bought in a cup, doused in vinegar, and devoured.

"It's a different generation," he said, hosing down the concrete floor around his stand one morning at 8:00. He had been up, as he is every morning, since 2:30. "Before, on Friday, Saturday, or Sunday, they had little barrows outside public houses, and in the markets with a bit of ice and jellied eels for sale, and the people queued up to buy. Now, kids can eat fast food at a different place every day. Six years ago, I was selling 2,200 dishes of jellied eels a week, and now I'm selling half that. In another six years, it'll be half again as few. And live eels? Forget it. There's probably not more than a dozen people in London buying live eels."

Still, Mick knew how to move eels. Every year, he said, he bought about 150 tons from the Lough Neagh Fishermen's Cooperative Society, as well as that many again from European eel farms. In addition to wholesaling them jellied to retailers, he provided them live to most of the restaurants and cafés in London that still had eel on the menu and got rid of about a half ton a week to Chinese buyers. If there was someplace to sell an eel in London, Mick Jenrick probably knew about it. He liked to say, "I may have a few peers in this business, but there's nobody above me."

The great value of farm-raised eels lies in the fact that they are all the same. The taste of a farm-raised eel is not quite as good as that of wild eels, admitted Mick, but it takes a discriminating *Anguilla*-phile's tongue to tell the difference, and with farm-raised animals an eel dealer can count on uniformity. Lough Neagh eels were virtually the only kind of wild eel that Mick sold any more. "They are the best eels in the world," he stated flatly.

"Fresh Shellfish & Jellied Eels" said the sign on the back wall of Vic Hollister's stall in the Chapel Market, a standard working-class outdoor market, lined with stalls selling everything from deodorant and shaving cream to fresh produce and fish, just a block away from the toney, gentrified Angel neighborhood in London's East End. The Chapel Market stretched for three long blocks down the middle of the street, and it encompassed 150 stalls. Vic, 46, was gray, grizzled, and affable, in a white apron, purely at home in his stall at the top of the street. The jellied eels referred to on the sign came from Mick's factory, and Vic swore by them.

"Look, I know my eels," he told me, in his thick, Cockney accent. "I was born and bred here, and baptized in the Islington Union Chapel. The East End used to be the best place in the world for eel. You had restaurants with a tank outside that had live eels in them; you picked the one you wanted to eat. They sold jellied eels, too. On Saturdays, there'd be a queue out the doors. Now there's less people selling eels in London every week."

Eels and shellfish had been good to Vic Hollister. There used to be three or four other stalls in the market where you could buy jellied eels, but his was the only one left. In the entire city, he estimated, there were a couple hundred places where you could still find eels for sale at a retail level. He owned a second home on land that he had bought 20 years ago in deep countryside, but where development was beginning to edge up toward his property, and he was thinking of looking for something quieter.

Vic was no friend to developers. He was an ex-president of the Chapel Market Merchants' Association, and while he was in office, a group of developers made a strong play to buy the area and close the market so they could replace it with hotels, flats, and sleek shopping. It cost the merchants' association £25,000 sterling and a lot of time and savvy media planning, he told me proudly, but they prevented the developers from closing them down.

His family had been at the Chapel Market since the 1860s. By the time Vic was seven, he was working with his father at the stand, lifting, carrying, stacking, learning how things functioned, making change, keeping counters wiped down and clean. "We worked hard, but we had a good time when I was a kid, too," he told me. "People knew how to enjoy themselves. In the summers my family would take off and go out in the country to pick hops: hopping. We slept in little wooden huts. At night they'd build a fire, pass around jugs of beer, sing and dance. Those were great summers."

Nevertheless, as he grew older, he decided he wanted to try doing something besides taking over the Chapel Market stall. He went to university and became an industrial engineer, with a family of his own. After more than a dozen years of it, he decided, when his father died, to come back to Fresh Shellfish and Jellied Eels; and watching the pleasure he got from talking to customers and the emotion with which he remembered defeating the development interests and saving the market, it was easy to see he had made the right choice.

Vic served his jellied eels in a white plastic foam cup like the kind in which you might get a take-out cup of coffee. He packed five chunks of eel in globs of gelatin inside and charged the equivalent of $3.00 for it. On the side of his stall was a small rack where he kept bottles of regular and hot vinegar for the customer to add; when his clients had their jellied eels seasoned to taste, he put a lid on the cup and off they went. He served the chunks of eel and gelatin out of one of Mick Jenrick's round, plastic 35-chunk bowls, the standard wholesale London size. It sat on a bed of ice alongside Vic's other staples—whelks, periwinkles, cockles, mussels, and frozen shrimp.

Despite its often-nasty weather, London is a city with a lot of outdoor markets, and on days when it is not raining they are full of people shopping. London's markets, in some cases, are nearly a thousand years old, and it will take more than supermarkets to deracinate the habit of shopping at them. One midday, as I was resting my elbow on Vic's counter, asking him questions and taking desultory notes, ceasing whenever a customer hove to, a harried-looking, middle-aged woman, rail-thin, stopped in front of Vic's stall and greeted him. She bought a cup of eels.

"It's for my father," she told me. "He can't get up and down the stairs so well anymore, but he has to have his eels for lunch, don't he? I've been buying my dad's eels here for ever so many years. I don't much care for them, and my kids won't eat them at all, but my dad's got to have them."

"Thanks, luv," Vic said to her, as she dug £1.80 out of a worn leather change purse and handed it over; then he turned back to me. "That's how it is these days. Only the old people still eat eels. The English have always eaten them, and during the last war, when most food was rationed, there were no rations for things that could be caught from the shore like eels, brown shrimps, and periwinkles.

"Everyone ate eel then, and glad to get it. Folks who are old now developed a real taste for them, but today it's only the poor and the old folks. Oh, down at some of these fancy restaurants that have set up in the Angel you'll get rich people coming into a fancy restaurant and eating a plate of eels. They say they're eating worker's food, just like a worker might go into a place and order lobster to eat rich people's food. But, there's less and less demand for it."

He recommended I walk down to Manze's at the other end of the market and try some of their "eel and mash," done the way it ought to be. I walked through the market to a store behind the stalls at the other end. It housed Manze's Eel and Pie House, and had done so for a long time by the look of the place. It was midday, and the queue was, indeed, out the door.

They were called eel and pie shops, or pie and mash shops. In 1995, there had been 87 of them scattered throughout greater London, according to the Pie 'N' Mash Club of Great Britain, a figure not greatly reduced from the 110 or so estimated to have been serving at the end of the 1800s. Many still had interiors with a nineteenth-century decor of dark wood and white tiles. Often, they seated customers on long wooden benches with backs, sharing a single long, wooden table. The menu was limited: meat pies or stewed eels, served with mashed potatoes in a big bowl, with a ladle of "liquor" from a big tin kettle poured over it, the liquor being a viscous sauce made from chopped parsley, water, and flour. To this, the customer added plain or hot vinegar from bottles on the counter. Devotees of pie houses were just as animated in their discussions of whether the liquor should be thick and dark green with parsley or thinner and lighter as Tiburcio Eskisabel Lukas was in talking about the best kind of olive oil in which to flash-fry his *angulas*. Pie and mash was a quintessential London working-class meal, but it was also served quickly and was filling, so many a London office worker lucky enough to be employed close to one went to a pie and mash shop for lunch.

The first eel pie shops were established in the mid-1700s, a famous one being the Eel Pie House, which began life as an inn on Twickenham Island in the River Thames. It was a favorite of pleasure boat parties on day outings from London, who would buy pies at the inn and picnic on them beside the river. The grand old inn ended its days occupied and "liberated" by hippies in the late 1960s.

Another well-known shop, with a reputation for good eel pies, was the Eel Pie House on New River in Highbury, built on the riverbank outside North London. It seems to have had a reputation for more than its eel pies, however. In the late 1700s, it was known for putting on such entertainments for its customers as dog fights and rat-killing matches. One writer of the time described its clientele as "the lowest order of people."

There have been public eating houses in London for many centuries, but a few hundred years ago, if people did not feel like cooking, they mostly got their prepared food from people with pushcarts. Just as produce was originally sold from pushcarts and outdoor stalls, before being moved under a market roof, so were victuals that a person could carry home. The streets of sixteenth-century London were full of people selling eel pies from small portable ovens. Eel was cheaper than meat; the Thames and other English rivers held plenty of them; and even eels that were imported aboard big Dutch trading ships were usually less expensive than home-grown beef or lamb. Fish, especially eel and cod, were a primary source of protein for the English, providing cheap, tasty, and plentiful fare.

Eels had also frequently graced the tables of the "better families" of medieval Europe, including England, for a number of reasons, not least of which was that nonmeat days as prescribed by the

Church calendar accounted for almost half the days in any given year. All Saturdays and Sundays, the 40 days of Lent, and a host of other saints' days and important dates on the religious calendar meant that fish would be the only flesh on the table for many meals during the year, and eel fit the bill.

In England, the earliest written collections of recipes included eels. Robert May included 16 eel recipes in his book *The Accomplisht Cook or the Art and Mystery of Cookery,* published in 1588. Roger May's father was a chef, and the son carried on the profession. In preparation, he was sent abroad. After five years working and studying in the great kitchens of Paris, he returned to England, still a young man, and went into service cooking for the English nobility until his retirement, a half century later, when he wrote his popular cookbook. In his preface, he asked the indulgence of those who did not like his volume: "It is impossible for any Authour to please all people, no more than the best cook can fancy their pallats whose mouths are alwayes out of taste."

Paris was already the place to which heads turned in western Europe when it came to noble cuisine, and the French have been eating eels since prehistoric times. Among the first ready-made foods sold in the streets of Paris, spiced pasties, small eel pies, were selling briskly by the mid-1200s. Eel dishes appear in the earliest French collections of recipes, including a fourteenth-century guide to keeping a household, written by an unknown Parisian and thought to have been published in late 1394, called *Menagier de Paris*. It contains a recipe for eel gruel.

In the early 1600s, the English Parliament enacted protectionist legislation banning the importation of fish, which gradually became scarcer and more expensive, causing an outcry among London's fishmongers and citizens. In 1680, an exception to the prohibition was requested in a petition before Parliament. The petition first called for the exception of cod, or stock-fish as it was called, because it was so important for preventing scurvy on board English commercial and military vessels. Then the case was made for eel, with eight reasons listed to show why allowing Dutch traders to bring eels into England would have positive results and benefit the nation. Among them were "that the aforesaid Trade of bringing live Eels into London Market, hath been practised time out of mind, as will appear by all the Ancient Mapps of the City of London where you will find the Eel-Ships always figured out in the River of Thames, lying at Anchor over against Queenbithe" and "that the said Live Eels are Esteemed (as in truth they are) most Excellent Food (The Price being set by the Right Honourable the Lord Mayor of London) . . . bought and sold, at very reasonable rates."

It was not too long before the protectionist barriers were removed and Dutch traders once again were bringing eels to England in live-haul sailing ships that could hold up to 6,000 pounds. Some of these eels were bought from eelers in Holland, but many of them were purchased in Denmark by Dutch merchants, then carried to London in ships with long tanks of muddy water built into their holds. The ships would anchor in the Thames, just offshore from the Billingsgate Fish Market, and from there customers could cheaply hire a small boat and oarsman and be rowed out to buy their eels from the Dutch in a lively, early morning river traffic.

Billingsgate was then, and still is, one of the world's most spectacular fish markets. What the Fulton Fish Market is to New York City and the Tsukiji market is to Tokyo, the Billingsgate Market is to London. The city's fish come through Billingsgate, and have since the Middle Ages. The market stood on the same spot in Thames Street, by the river, for over 400 years before being moved to new quarters in 1998, when London's Docklands area was built and the market relocated there in a huge, low, brick building at waterside. In a nineteenth-century paean to the market, in his book *The Food of London,* George Dodd wrote:

It has seen out the Normans and the Plantagenets, the Lancasters and the Yorkists, the Tudors and the Stuarts, the Orangists and the Georges; it has supplied fish to all of them. It has witnessed great fires, great plagues, gilded barges, river pageants, Tower executions, City insurrections, custom-houses new and old, London Bridge with houses and without; and yet there it is still. Beling's Gate supplied the old city in 1055, as Billingsgate now supplies the monster metropolis in 1855.

For all those years, one of the staples offered for sale was eel. By the late 1700s, city records show that over 3.5 million pounds of it were moving through Billingsgate each year. Less than a century later, that number was down to just below 2 million pounds of eel sold at Billingsgate in 1850, according to Henry Mayhew's 1851 book *London Labour and the London Poor.* That is still a lot of eels, and among the people who bought them at Billingsgate on any given morning in the mid-1800s, one would have found inn and restaurant cooks, housewives, and those who cooked for the households of the rich and great. There would also have been hordes of the familiar piemen, who sold their wares from portable warming ovens on the street over the course of a day. Such street vendors of cheap food and clothing were called costermongers, and they were frequently Cockneys, or, often, Jews. They were pressed on all sides. The police arrested them at whim, because they did not have licenses, but to remove them entirely from the streets would have put basic goods beyond the reach of the poor, who could not afford to buy indoors, where prices were higher. The coster had to pay rent each morning for a barrow or portable oven, which he or she would then take to a market—Billingsgate, for the eel sellers—and fill with produce. The day would be spent moving through the streets, crying their wares—"Eels O! Eels O! Alive! Alive O!"—until their stock was gone or it was too late to sell anymore. Often, they would have had to borrow the money to pay for their eels in Billingsgate at the beginning of the day, and if bad weather or other unforeseeable circumstances held down their sales, they could end the day owing money. In addition to those who hawked eel pies, there were other street vendors offering stewed eels in "liquor."

Not all the odds were against the vendors, however. Some 3,000 costermongers bought fish and eels every morning at Billingsgate, and they had their ways of cutting costs. Dead eels were cheaper than live, and Mayhew reported that many a costermonger mixed his eels 20 pounds of dead to 5 pounds of living, and in so doing considered that he had done fairly by his customers. After all, the eel in an eel pie had to be killed before being cooked, they reasoned, and if some had been dead a few hours longer than others, taste was not likely to be affected. Particularly scrupulous dealers bragged that they used equal parts dead and live eels, according to Mayhew. Such business practices by street vendors may have gained eels a somewhat dubious reputation but do not seem to have diminished the collective appetite for them or to have had a negative impact on sales.

What with so many people in so many places around the world catching everything from elvers to silver eels, it is amazing that any of them live out their full lives, but many do. They enter fresh water as glass eels and head upstream to spend years growing slowly, passing voracious summers hunting at night and torpid winters burrowed in the mud. The average age when eels make the transition from yellow to silver is thought to be around nine or ten years, but it can be a lot longer than that. Systematic capture of silver eels returning to the Sargasso, carried out over the course of 1987 and 1988 in the Burrishoole River in western Ireland, for instance, found that eels moving downriver had an age range of between 8 and 57 years old. Fifty-seven years is a long time to wait to reproduce in any species. There was an eel in Sweden so famous it had a name, Putte, which was caught at what was estimated to be the age of 3 and lived to be 88, spending its last years in an aquarium at the Salsingburg Museum, according to Christopher Moriarty in *Eels: A Natural and Unnatural History;* an albino eel was kept in an aquarium in Trocadero, Spain, from 1913 to 1946, Léon Bertin records in *Eels: A Biological Study;* and there are numerous other records, virtually everywhere eels are found, of eels occasionally reaching an exceptionally advanced age. These long-lived eels are frequently found in an apparently inaccessible body of water, and they are invariably females.

Male eels not only are about half the size of adult females but also almost never go far upriver. They congregate in areas of brackish water and seem to spend most of their lives there before, theoretically, going back to the Sargasso to mate. It is generally accepted that there are some males that never enter fresh water. Whether all the males make a return journey to the Sargasso is unknown. The females, however, keep going upriver for incredible distances. What draws them on, and how do they know when they have reached the place to stop and spend the next 8 or 10 or 20 years? No human has a clue.

Virtually all of the eels past a certain upriver point will be females, and it is believed that the eel's sexual characteristics do not develop until the journey begins. There is a period in a young eel's life when it is, apparently, hermaphroditic, with the potential to develop into either a male or a female. Scientific evidence seems to indicate that in places where food is plentiful and the population density is low, most of the eels will be thriving females. If eels are kept crowded together in ponds with no escape, the vast majority of them will be males.

The eels moving upstream are on a determined search for optimum living conditions. There is no evidence to indicate that eels return to the same body of fresh water where their mothers lived. "We still can't absolutely preclude that, but if there was a substantial degree of return to an area where their parents came from, one would expect to see genetic differentiation occurring," said James McCleave, of the University of Maine. "For salmon, each river has a genetic stock that's a little bit different from the next one, and you can examine that salmon and tell what river it was spawned in.

"All the evidence that we have for eels suggests that there's a mingling on the spawning grounds and, presumably, random or nearly random mating among males and females from anywhere, and pretty much a stochastic [random] distribution of the offspring. It's a little difficult to postulate a return to a specific body of fresh water, because these larvae are starting out tiny and growing slowly, and they don't have much muscle, so expecting them to have a swimming behavior capable of overcoming currents and eddies to get back to a particular spot is not a parsimonious explanation. The genetic evidence and lack of swimming capability of the larvae make us pretty sure it's random distribution."

Whatever it is that tells a young eel it has finally reached its home body of fresh water, the animal's basic demands are certainly not high-rent. All it asks for is a river or lake with a muddy bottom, preferably with rocks, crevices, plenty of hidey-holes, and an ample food source. Simple things, but an eel keeps going until they are found. A certain part of any given year's elvers will stay behind to hang around the estuary for the rest of their freshwater days, but another part of the group will head upriver, moving forward at any cost, toward a promised land. Eel biologists say that those that stay behind around the fresh/salt water mix have "low migratory drive." And those that forge on, swimming and eating by night, resting by day, display "high migratory drive."

Call it what you will, but those eels with high migratory drive are in the grip of a serious urge. They are quite willing to cross land to reach a body of water so that they can continue their journey and are thought capable of going a mile or two overland, which explains their presence in landlocked lakes and ponds. They are built about as well for surviving on land as any known fish. They have small gills, and the coating of mucous that covers their bodies keeps their skins moist enough to breathe through. A significant part of an eel's respiratory process is carried out through its skin. An eel that finds shelter during the day in mud, or under damp leaves, can stay out of water as long as two days before dying.

That eels will cross land to reach water is well-documented, but whether they stop to eat on such a journey, or leave the water for the express purpose of eating, is unknown. Arguments on both sides of the question have been put forward for nearly 500 years. Many writers have held that eels do come ashore to feed, beginning with Albertus Magnus—by no means an unimpeachable source, as he was also the first grand partisan of a live-birth theory of eel reproduction. He wrote, "The eel also comes out of the water in the night-time into the fields, where he can find pease, beans, or lentils."

George Brown Goode's report on eels in his 1884 study of U.S. fisheries quoted a writer named Bach who, a century earlier, in a book entitled *The Natural History of East and West Prussia,* repeated the same calumny about eels raiding pea patches, asserting the charge as bald fact. Bach wrote:

> These movements explain the paradoxical fact that in Prussia and Pomerania fish have been caught upon dry land by the use of the plow, for the peasants, in warm nights when the Eels are in search of the pease, towards morning when it is not yet day make furrows with the plow between them and the water, and these are the nets in which the Eels are caught. Since the Eel moves with ease only upon the grass, its return to the water is cut off by the soil which has been thrown up.

Some of these old reports have a slightly alarmist tone to them, as if the eels intended to colonize dry land or systematically raid crops. None is more worrisome, however, than a *Wall Street Journal* report from September 2000 about the appearance of Asian swamp eels in South Florida. This story was not unlike reports that had surfaced a few years earlier about walking catfish, another mud dweller. Biologists warned that the swamp eel, which had never before been reported in the United States, was likely to eat everything in sight and devastate the local fish populations. Furthermore, the scientists warned that they were incredibly tough and resistant—an Asian swamp eel was reported to have lived seven months in a damp towel.

The contention that eels might come ashore in search of food has been debated for a long time. Many have disputed the notion, among them such exceptionally talented observers as the great Italian natural historian Lazare Spallanzani, who wrote about eels in Lake Comacchio at the end of the eighteenth century. He noted that at the lake, site of Italy's most productive eel fishery, no fisherman had ever reported seeing an eel on land, and, furthermore, that once when the lake dried up greatly and many eels died, none of them made an effort to cross land and reach the nearby Po River.

Once an eel, for whatever reasons, has decided on a stretch of water in which to pass her freshwater life, she will burrow in, going out at night to hunt when the weather—and thus the water—is warm, and remaining in a torpid, near-dormant state during winter in those places where the water temperature drops below 10°C (50°F). When it is that cold, the eel exists in a state of virtual hibernation, down in the mud with the catfish and other bottom-feeders, and does not eat. When the water warms to 14°C (57°F), it begins to eat. And, as the water continues warming, the eel turns into a voracious, no-nonsense carnivore, preying on just about anything alive that crosses its path and will fit in its relatively small mouth, as well as recently dead things. Eels have a reputation as eaters of dead things, but the truth is that during experiments they have consistently chosen to starve in aquariums rather than eat carrion, and eelers know that any dead fish or crabs they use as bait in their pots must be freshly killed. It is possible that an eel in the wild would eat something long dead if there was nothing else available, but it would certainly be a last resort.

Part of eels' unsavory reputation comes from the fact that they are frequently present on drowned corpses. Perhaps the single most dominant Western literary image of eels is a scene vividly painted by the German writer Günter Grass, in his novel *The Tin Drum*. While little Oskar (the book's hero), his parents, and his mother's lover watch, a fisherman using a freshly killed horse's head as bait laboriously pulls the head into shore so he can pick the eels off it. It is a scene filled with both comedy and revulsion. First, the fisherman takes a couple of dozen smaller eels off the head. Next, he begins to squeeze it and bigger, darker eels ooze out. Then, Grass writes:

> With the help of his rubber boot he wrenched the horse's mouth open and forced a club between the jaws, so that the great yellow horse teeth seemed to be laughing. And when the longshore-

man—only now did I see he was bald as an egg—reached both hands into the horse's gullet and pulled out two at once, both of them as thick and long as a man's arm, my mother's jaws were also torn asunder: she disgorged her whole breakfast, pouring out lumpy egg white and threads of egg yolk mingled in lumps of bread soaked in café au lait over the stones of the breakwater.

(trans. Ralph Manheim, 1961)

If a freshly killed horse's head should sink down in front of it, an eel would be pleased to take a bite, according to marine biologists, but the meal would be the equivalent of a cold, leftover chicken leg in the refrigerator: something to appease hunger. What an eel really likes to eat is one of the relatively few things about the animal that human observers have catalogued with some exactitude. Over the years, thousands of eels have been sacrificed so that their stomach contents could be examined. While their diet varies greatly depending on location, its components usually consist of things that were alive when the eel ate them, generally small crustaceans, snails, insect larvae, and fish. When available, shad roe is always a favorite, as North Carolina eelers like Gary Koonce know well, and the kinds of insects that frequent lakes, rivers, and ponds seem to figure often as filler. Water striders and mayfly nymphs are typical insect prey for eels, as are minnows and mussels, caddis fly eggs and crawfish, small snails and midges. Of course, an eel not only eats, but is frequently eaten. *Anguilla* play an important part in the aquatic food chain. They are eaten by larger fish, and water fowl such as ducks, herons, and egrets devour eels with great gusto.

Eels will also eat each other, at least in captivity, even if there is other food available. In an experiment carried out in the aquarium of the Jardin des Plantes in Paris, in 1937, 1,000 elvers, caught in that same year, were put in water. Meat and other foodstuffs were provided for them, but a year later only 71 eels remained in the tank, and two months later there were only 12 survivors. The rest had not died natural deaths, but had been devoured by their roommates. Within another two months, a single eel remained in the tank, a female, who disappeared from record some years later during the Second World War, according to Léon Bertin.

Eels have small, blunt teeth that can grasp but are not able to do much in the way of cutting. Eels will bite, but only as a last resort. A small eel's bite is about like the rasp of fine sandpaper on a finger. Large eels, however, have powerful jaws, and an eel's chomp can open a wound. Those who separate out the eels on the grading tables at the Lough Neagh Fishermen's Cooperative plant, for instance, say that if a big one clamps down on an errant finger while she is being lifted up to toss her into a barrel, the wound heals slowly. However, eels would rather flee than fight every time; their preferred mode of dealing with a threat is always by escape, and they are as well equipped for it as any animal in the world. It is an ever-surprising experience to try and grasp an eel, an amazing sensation of otherworldly slipperiness.

The eel is considerably limited in what it can eat by the reptile-like shape of its head, its underslung jaw and small mouth looking as if they would be more at home on a snake or a turtle than on a fish. If a prey is too large to swallow whole, eels have to resort to ripping and tearing. They do so in a most unusual manner, taking full advantage of their supple bodies. An eel will grasp the prey in its jaws and begin to spin around the axis of its own body, tearing away flesh as it does so. Eels have been measured, in captivity, spinning their bodies at upward of 14 rotations per second, according to a 1995 article in *Nature*. To get an idea of how fast that is, consider that figure skaters, who probably spin as rapidly as any human beings, achieve only about five rotations a second on their best days.

Eels are generally portrayed as rapacious when they are hunting for food, but other than that they seem to be pretty mild-mannered, sedentary homebodies. Eels implanted with tiny radio transmitters, and tracked for months, stay within a few hundred yards of wherever they spend their dormant days and hunting nights. Once they have made their choice of a place to live, after so much traveling, they appear to settle right in and not to wander. The same kind of tiny, implanted radio transmitters have been used to show that eels captured in one place and released in another generally return to the place from which they were taken. Scientists have transported and released them ten miles away from where they were taken, and while it took many of them a week or more to do it, they usually returned to the place where they were captured.

It is, perhaps, not surprising that an animal capable of setting out from coastal waters on a journey to the Sargasso Sea is endowed with superb navigational abilities. In fact, an eel's homing instinct and directional sense are among its most remarkable and least understood qualities, according to James McCleave. "There's been speculation and a little bit of experimentation that maybe they have an ability to sense the earth's magnetic field and use it as a compass reference like we would. That's a mechanism that might be behind this directional sense. They seem to be able to return to areas after displacement. Tesch and some of his colleagues did early tagging work in the North Sea that suggested eels return to areas of previous capture from considerable distances."

I have never liked being asked to identify myself by someone who is holding a gun on me, and I enjoy it even less when it happens on open water. But such was my experience on what had been an otherwise extremely pleasant morning on Lough Neagh, sunny and warm, in stark contrast to the lake's usual preponderance of gray, rainy days. I was with Bill McElroy, who was behind the wheel of his patrol boat—a 30-foot fiberglass runabout with a small cabin up front and a powerful Volvo Penta diesel engine—working the day shift for the Lough Neagh Fishermen's Cooperative Society. He made sure that all the regulations were obeyed, passing around the lake from boat to boat, stopping to talk to eelers about how the fishing was going, and radioing his sense of how large the day's catch might be back to Father Kennedy at the plant so he could begin to get an idea of how many eels might be expected to arrive later that morning in the live-haul trucks.

Suddenly, from out of nowhere, two big, rubber Zodiac-type boats appeared, one on either side of us, each powered by a pair of 140-horsepower Suzuki outboards, with a machine gun mounted on a gunwale, and each carrying three uniformed British soldiers. They were young and had mean, closed faces. In each boat, one of the soldiers was behind the mounted gun, leveling it in our direction, another was behind the wheel of the boat, and the third held in his hands an automatic rifle, pointed at us. The rifleman in the rubber boat on our port side barked, "Names?"

At 55, Bill McElroy was a solidly built man with a sharp nose, close-cut black hair gone mostly gray, and a bit of a paunch that he attributed to having quit smoking two packs a day a few years before. He had six kids, and he had been patrolling Lough Neagh for the fishermen's cooperative for 17 years. His paunch was not noticeable as he stood ramrod straight at the wheel of the boat, idling its engine in neutral, looking dead ahead, never glancing at the boats to either side. "William McElroy," he spoke in an even voice to the air in front of him.

I followed suit, and tried to keep my voice steady when I called out my name, despite the mixture of anger and fear that kept my eyes locked on the machine gun pointed at me across a couple yards of water. The drivers of the two boats nodded at each other, slipped into gear, and roared off across the water, leaving us rocking in their wakes. "They are out here stopping boats quite often," he told me afterward. "They can come in your house without a warrant; you can be arrested and held indefinitely without charges."

It was not pleasant to be bullied at gunpoint by the equivalent of British football hooligans, swaggering, stupid youngsters, kitted out in uniforms, with lots of firepower. But, the Special Powers Act, passed in 1922, made such bullying possible, and people have gotten used to it. They don't allow it to ruin their appetites. Bill's patrol had started at dawn, and by 10 A.M. we had already been out on the water for more than four hours, so Bill decided it was time to for breakfast. Over the course of the morning's visits with various boats, he had asked for an eel here and an eel there, and he now had five smallish ones curled up at the bottom of a bucket, muddy-green coiled bodies, small unblinking fish eyes with golden irises.

Typical Lough Neagh eels, he said, as he spread some pages of old newspaper on the patrol boat's transom and proceeded to have all five of them cleaned in about ten minutes. First, he opened them with a fillet knife and scooped out the guts, tossing them overboard, much to the pleasure of a flock of black-headed gulls that instantly appeared. Then, he made a light incision nearly all around the head, slid the knife between the skin and flesh, and peeled the skin right away in a practiced movement, leaving perfectly skinned eels behind. These he cut up in two-inch strips, saving a somewhat bigger piece of one of the eels to rub on the bottom of the large skillet in which he cooked them. He laid some 20 pieces of eel carefully in the big, use-blackened pan, on a two-burner gas camping stove, and we sat in the boat's cramped, shadowy cabin for an hour, sipping tea, as the eels cooked slowly, simmering in their own juice. "The thing about Lough Neagh eels that makes them so special and appreciated is that they have such a high fat content," he told me. "You don't even need to put any oil in the pan to fry them. You can't cook eels from other places dry like that. They just don't have the fat."

After about 45 minutes, Bill cut raw onion slices and put them in the skillet on top of the eel. He covered the skillet, letting the eels cook for another 15 minutes while he buttered some soda bread and poured another cup of tea. The pieces of eel came out golden brown, soft, flaky, and delicious, with a light, rich, fish taste. We ate with our fingers, ten pieces of eel each, mopped up the eel oil with the bread, and wiped our greasy hands on old newspapers. It was a mighty breakfast, rich and tasty, and by 11:30 we were done and resting on deck a moment before kicking over the engine to go back on patrol. Engine off, adrift on the lake, we sat replete, with Lough Neagh flies clouded around our heads. To the east were the Mourne Mountains; otherwise, the horizon revealed only flat, verdant pasture, tableland, sloping gently toward the water. "Well," Bill sighed, "that's the highlight of the day. It's all downhill from here."

Almost, anyway. In elver season, the other favorite part of Bill McElroy's day came at the end of it, the last daily duty he performed before calling it quits for his shift. After the patrol boat was gassed up and turned over to whoever was going out next, he turned his attention to elvers. He climbed in his truck and drove 20 miles to the traps at the mouth of the Bann in Colerane. On the way, he often stopped at Carn Row, where there was a low spillway built across a large part of the river. For the convenience of elvers that got beyond the traps at Colerane, Bill had laid a pair of thick straw ropes, some 15 yards of braided straw, leading up from the river to the top of the spillway and the continuation of the Bann. Eel ladders made of straw are ancient devices for catching elvers in a number of places in Europe. Bill lifted up the braided straw and found hundreds of elvers clinging to its underside, making their slow way up it toward Lough Neagh. These Bill put in a pail, which he dumped into the tank on the back of his truck. His next stop was the elver traps in Colerane, where he was taking 10,000–12,000 a night to add to the tank. His last job of the day was to return to Lough Neagh, back the truck down to the water, and run a hose from the truck's tank to the lake. Through it, he delivered the evening's haul of elvers, and another crop of Lough Neagh eels was planted.

That hour spent capturing elvers and releasing them in the lake saved each of the elvers an entire dangerous year spent ascending the Bann. "All the Lough Neagh eelers see me doing is patrolling, and enforcing the regulations, but working with elvers is the part of the job where I feel like I'm really doing some good," he told me. "Sometimes I just wish they at least had some idea we do this every day. For me, it's the most satisfying."

Bill McElroy admitted that he would rather be eeling, himself, than patrolling. That was what he did before he took the job with the cooperative, 17 years ago. But, with six kids, payments on his new and ample home, and a host of other obligations, he felt that a regular paycheck was a necessary thing at this point in his life. His oldest daughter was a nurse, and his oldest son was preparing to graduate from the university with a degree in chemistry. Bill himself grew up with eeling as his only possible future.

His father was one of the original group of desperate eelers who had come to Oliver Kennedy for help in 1963, on a day that the priest still remembered well. "Bill's father had 13 children, six boys and seven girls, living in a small house on the shores of the lough, and his income was minimal," Kennedy told me. "How he succeeded in looking after all those children, only the Lord knows.

"Originally, Bill was fishing like his father. Then, when we had some problems, he undertook to go on the protection staff, and he has been at that for 17 years. He has made a major contribution to the fishery and the fishermen here by what he's doing. That's to his credit. His boy is graduating from the university next Monday; he has raised a fine family and lives in a nice home. It's encouraging to see that happening. That's the kind of thing that gives me a certain personal sense of satisfaction."

CHAPTER 5

Yankee
Eels

In North America, the eel has suffered a precipitous decline in popularity, and it is not easy to get a fix on why. People along the Atlantic seaboard continued to include it regularly in their diets through the nineteenth century and well into the twentieth. Yet, after the Second World War it virtually disappeared from the table, and most North Americans who now live where eels abound will pass their whole lives without tasting them. This would be unthinkable all over Europe, from Italy up to Sweden and from England across to Bulgaria, but the only steady domestic market left in the United States is in cities with large Asian populations, and that market is too small to support much of a fishery. Eel has disappeared from the national menu.

"Nobody is cooking like they used to, and least of all cooking eel," Barry Kratchman, president of Delaware Valley Seafood, said during a dinner he treated me to at Bookbinder's, a lovely, century-old Philadelphia restaurant of brass and wood, noted for its seafood. Eel was not on the menu, but oysters, small, tasty steamer clams, crab, and squid were, and Kratchman ordered a little of everything.

"Even the young Italians don't make the old eel dishes, anymore. Maybe at Christmas somebody in the family might fix eel, but fewer and fewer. It's just like my mother making her own gefilte fish. People don't do that anymore, either.

"Don't worry about the price, the company's paying," he said, as we read through the menu. Delaware Valley Seafood was the Philadelphia competition that Martie Bouw worried about incessantly, and Barry Kratchman, 36, was the third generation to be competing with Holland Seafood. His grandfather, David, had been a truck driver, transporting eels in the late 1960s for Superior Fish Company, a Philadelphia firm that no longer exists. He decided he had what it takes to be an eel distributor instead of just driving for one, so he quit and set up his own business. No one wanted eel domestically in those days either, but the European demand was high. "Back in the 1970s, eels were everywhere," Barry Kratchman told me. "We could send three trucks out a week and pick up ten or fifteen thousand pounds of eel in each one. And, we could sell them."

Barry's father, Sheldon, ran the buying and selling from the Philadelphia offices, and his grandfather continued to drive a truck, but for his own company. He died in an accident, at age 62, at the wheel of a Delaware Valley live-haul truck, and Sheldon was left with the business. Barry started working with his father in 1990, and in 1993 they moved Delaware Valley Seafood from a building in downtown Philadelphia to nearby Norristown, where they had 30 tanks for adult eels, including 17 large tanks, each of which held 1,000 gallons. In 1999, his father retired, and Barry became president of the company.

Who, I asked him, was the man known as Cigar to down east North Carolina eelers like Gary Koonce? He turned out to be a man who had driven Delaware Valley trucks for many years and had a taste for cigars. He was retired. "Cigar is a great guy," said Kratchman. "We used to send him down South to get a hotel room, call the eelers, and say he was in their area ready to buy eels. He's a real character."

Barry was a bachelor and lived in a lovely apartment in a luxurious waterfront development. There were Escher prints on his wall and wrinkled gym clothes on the floor. He was tanned, with dark hair combed back and alert blue eyes. Clean-shaven, short and fit, with a compact muscular body. He told me that he liked to take a month off every so often and hike, for example, the Cordillera mountain range between Chile and Argentina.

Over the ten years he had been buying and selling eels, the market for adult eels had grown tighter and tighter. The combination of a strong dollar and a lot of farm-raised eels available in Europe meant that European buyers had drastically cut back on their orders of American eels. "When I started working with my father, we were doing over a million pounds a year, and my grandfather may have done as much as 2 million. Now we'd be lucky to do half a million a year. We've had to diversify into other live products like tilapia and striped bass. In the last few years we've been dealing with farm-raised fish. There are going to be a lot of changes in the eel business in the next couple of years. I can't tell you about them now, they're still confidential, but believe me there are going to be some changes."

I asked him how much competition Holland Seafood was for Delaware Valley? Were the two companies equally important to the U.S. eel market? "I'm not going to talk about specifics, but there are going to be some big changes soon. I'm just not ready to talk about them."

The European market may be shrinking, but it is still a market. After all, the half million pounds that Delaware Valley sells to Europe is about 1.5 million eels. So, why is it that twenty-first-century Europeans still hunger for the taste of eel and stateside diners do not? It is, frankly, hard to imagine adequate reasons, hard to find one that carries any weight other than generalities about how they look too much like snakes, or are mud-foragers, or some other equally vague explanation, not nearly good enough reasons to lose a cultural taste for such a delicious and common fish. That other bottom-feeder, the catfish, has been exalted as North America's premium farm-raised fish, while eel has been cast aside. Why should such scorn be heaped on *Anguilla rostrata?* Eel was, after all, among the founding foods of the United States and, along with corn, cod, turkey, and deer, it fed the *Mayflower* Pilgrims.

One hundred and two people left England for the New World in September 1620 aboard the *Mayflower*. Since no white people had previously settled in New England, the *Mayflower*'s passengers had no precedents on which to base their planning, and they managed to do almost everything wrong, beginning with the decision to leave in the autumn. On December 11, they made landfall at Plymouth Rock in the dead of a New England winter. They were clumsy, God-distracted townspeople, unskilled at fishing or hunting, accustomed to buying their eels and all the rest of their food at the market. The men managed to kill a few birds and gathered some mussels. They were flummoxed, pole-axed, overwhelmed, in shock as the reality of their self-imposed exile outside the pale of civilization sank in, huddled together trying to keep warm, praying, unable to quite provide for themselves, terrified of the imagined savages lurking unseen in the surrounding woods. Fever, malnutrition, death were all around, fear of the unknown pervaded their every waking moment, an undercurrent to everything they did.

By spring, nearly half their number were dead. The rest would have likely followed them into the grave, or returned to England, but they were saved by a Native American so large-spirited that he was willing to help them, even though other English had captured and sold him and had brought the influenza that had wiped out his tribe. In the early 1600s, Tisquantum, known in Euro-American history books as Squanto, was captured by Englishmen who lured him and 16 other Pawtuxets on board the ship with which they were exploring the New World's coast. He eventually served years in virtual slavery to an English merchant ship owner. When he finally got back to his homeland in 1619, he found his tribe's villages gone, not a Pawtuxet left living, all wiped out by a disease the English had introduced. He was the last Pawtuxet. He went to live with the neighboring Wampanoag tribe.

In March 1621, he presented himself to the *Mayflower* colonists, along with Samoset, a Wampanoag. Tisquantum spoke English. It was, after all, the tongue of the people who had kidnapped him into servitude. He knew all about the dark side of the English, but he was still merciful enough to open the land and water to the Plymouth settlers, to read them the North American book of survival in their own language. Tisquantum was the first real American hero of record, a forgiving, compassionate human being. He gave the Plymouth colony his grain—corn—and the secrets of growing it. He taught them how to hunt meat and harvest wild vegetables, which fruits and berries were edible, and how to fish. And the first thing he showed the colonists was how to fish for eels. On April 4, 1621, according to John Goodwin's *The Pilgrim Republic:* "Samoset and Tisquantum were still guests of the Colony. In the afternoon, the latter went to Eel River, apparently, and by treading in the mud caught, with his hands alone, as many fat, sweet eels as he could bring back to his entertainers." It was not long before the colonists were treading up eels themselves.

One of the earliest English travel writers to publish an account of his voyage to the New World was John Josselyn, son of a knight. His father had fallen on hard times in the early 1600s and had been forced to sell his ancestral manor. Josselyn's older brother, Henry, having few prospects at home in England, settled in New England about the same time that the *Mayflower* settlers arrived at Plymouth. Henry Josselyn was wholly loyal to the Crown, and he eventually attained the office of Lieutenant Governor of the Province of Maine. The *Mayflower* colonists wanted nothing to do with him. His feelings toward them were the same. He laid claim to a vast tract of Maine, and it was to visit his older brother there that John Josselyn undertook a two-year voyage in 1638. He returned to Maine in 1663 and stayed until 1671, when he went back to England for the last time and wrote *Two Voyages To New England,* published in 1675. He recorded: "The Eal is of two sorts, salt-water Eals and fresh water Eals, these again are distinguished into yellow bellied Eals and silver bellied Eals; I never eat better Eals in no part of the world that I have been in, than are here. They that have no mind or leasure to take them, may buy of an Indian half a dozen silver bellied Eals as big as those we usually give 8 pence or 12 pence a piece for at London, for three pence."

Native Americans had been eeling for centuries, as evidenced by Josselyn's advice that those who were disinclined to go eeling for themselves buy their eels from an Indian. And at prices far below those of Billingsgate. (Ah, the joys of traveling to foreign lands and buying delicacies cheap.) Two of England's most consumed fishes—cod and eel—were there waiting for the colonists. Cod so thick it was said a person could walk to shore across their backs, and eels swarming in the rivers and bays for the taking.

William Wood wrote in *New Englands Prospect,* published in 1634, that the Indians of Massachusetts made great use of the local eels: "There be a great store of Salt water eeles, especially in such places where grass growes: for to take these there be certaine Eele pots, which must be baited with a peece of Lobster, into which the Eeles entring cannot returne backe againe: some take a bushell in a night in this manner, eating as many as they neede of for the present, and salt up the rest against winter. These eeles be not so luscious a taste as they be in England . . . but are both wholesome for the body, and delightfull for the taste."

Jesuit missionaries in New York found the Iroquois consuming eels as a staple in their diet. The Iroquois particularly liked to spit eels on twigs and grill them over a fire, much as the Italians loved to do during the Middle Ages with their eels at Lake Comacchio, the large body of estuarine water below Venice, then and now Italy's prime eel fishing grounds. The Algonquin tribes smoked them, just as the Dutch, Germans, and Scandinavians were doing at the same time across the Atlantic.

A popular way to prepare eels among Native Americans across New England was in a thick fish soup. In his *Historical Account of the Indians,* first published in 1677, Daniel Gookin wrote: "Their food is generally boiled maize, or Indian corn, mixed with kidney-beans, or sometimes without. Also they frequently boil in this pottage, fish and flesh of all sorts, either new taken or dried, as shads, eels, alewives, or a kind of herring. . . . These they cut in pieces, bones and all, and boil them in the aforesaid pottage."

Waverly Root wrote that among northeastern Indians there was a "fish soup from which the fish had disappeared before the dish was served, like a French *soupe de poisson,* described summarily as 'fish of any kind boiled in a quantity of water. It is then removed and coarse corn siftings stirred in to make a soup of suitable consistency.' The Indians called it *u'nega'gei.*" Root does not comment on the similarity between this Native American word and the Japanese word for eel, *unagi.*

Eel rapidly became a staple in the colonists' diet. One of the basic ways the Pilgrims prepared it was as an "eel stifle," and an eel stifle is still occasionally served on the Massachusetts island of Martha's Vineyard, or found in New England cookbooks. It is basically potatoes and onions layered with eel in a pot, with a little flour between the layers. On top is some salt pork and pork fat. Water is added, nearly to cover, and the whole shebang is cooked until the meats are firm but tender. Early settlers in New England quickly learned to take advantage of the annual run of silver eels downriver to the ocean. Smoked meat was what saw them through the long winters, and smoked eel could be found in most households. In *The Yankee Cookbook,* Imogene Wolcott quotes an unidentified New Hampshire poet writing about the relationship of the state's colonists to eels:

> From the eels they formed their food in chief,
> And eels were called the Derryfield beef;
> It was often said that their only care,
> And their only wish and their only prayer,
> For the present world and the world to come,
> Was a string of eels and a jug of rum.

After the Revolution and statehood, the same calumny was applied to citizens of other states. There was a saying that all it took to make someone from Rhode Island happy was "a jug of rum and a mess of eels."

As time went on, and the denizens of the new republic started making money and forming villages, towns, and cities, they apparently retained their taste for eel. It remained a common and popular food up and down the eastern seaboard. Eels turn up in the first cookbook of American authorship, *American Cookery,* the writer of which, Amelia Simmons, described herself as "an American orphan." The book was published in 1796 in Hartford, Connecticut, and recommends that eels be so fresh that they jump when they are dropped in the pan to fry. Over 50 years later, in 1849, Henry David Thoreau echoed her, calling the eel of the Merrimac River: "a slimy, squirming creature, informed of mud, still squirming in the pan, speared and hooked up with various success."

In the early 1800s, eels from the Pettaquamscutt River in Rhode Island, caught by being speared in the mud under the ice where they wintered, held a special place on the menu, according to Thomas Robinson Hazard of Narragansett, Rhode Island. Hazard, a minister, wrote a book, *The Jonnycake Papers,* about life in the early nineteenth century, when he was a child. With the following description of a winter morning's breakfast, from sometime around 1810, he leaves no doubt that eels were much appreciated in his privileged part of the world:

> The glorious excellence of these eel, prepared in the old time way, I am sure no poet — not even Homer or Byron, with all their glowing powers of description — can portray, much less a simple writer of prose. The method was as follows: A basket of fresh, yellow-breasted eels being brought fresh from the frozen river, were first saturated with a handful of wood ashes. This loosened the coating of slime so that they were readily cleansed. Next the head was taken off, and the eel split down the entire length of the back. They were then washed in clean sea water and hung up the kitchen chimney, with its wide, open fireplace, for one night only. Next morning, the eels were cut in short pieces and

placed on a gridiron, flesh side next to sweet-smelling, glowing coals, made from green oak, walnut, or maple wood. When sufficiently broiled on that side, they were turned on the gridiron and a small slice of fragrant butter, made from the milk of cows fed on honey-laden white clover and aromatic five-fingers, put on each piece of eel. By this time the family were seated at the breakfast table in the great room, waiting impatiently for the all-but-divine luxury, the exquisite aroma of which penetrated every nook and cranny of the house. In due time it appears, on a China plate, you may say; by no means! But on the identical gridiron, hot and luscious, with little transparent globules of dew-like nectar sparkling on each piece. Every guest or member of the family helps himself from the hot gridiron, which is then returned again to the glowing coals, and again and again replenished until their appetite is surfeited or the supply of eels exhausted. . . .

There used to be an old man in Narragansett by the name of Scribbins, who was a great favorite of my grandfather because of his simplicity and honesty. When a small boy, I remember Scribbins breakfasting at our house, one winter morning, when we had broiled eels. The old man helped himself from the gridiron seventeen times, a steady smile playing over his features every moment that passed between the first and last mouthful. He then looked my grandfather blandly and steadily in the face, and significantly nodding his head sideways in the direction of the kitchen door, remarked: "Them's eels, them is."

The nation's first big-selling cookbook, the one that set the standard for those to follow for many a year, was Mary Randolph's *The Virginia Housewife,* first published in 1824, when its author was 62 years old. Randolph's father was Thomas Jefferson's foster brother, and the two grew up in the same house. Mary Randolph married a man who owned a Virginia tobacco plantation, and, later, she was the proprietor of a Richmond boardinghouse. For the sake of propriety, she refused to allow her name to appear in the first edition of her cookbook, preferring to be just another anonymous Virginia housewife; but when the book quickly sold out and was reprinted, she added her name. It went through six editions in all. It contained the first recipe for beaten biscuits and three for eel: grilled, broiled, and "pitchcocked," meaning the eels were skewered through their length, laid across a grill, and served as a kind of eel kebab, much as the Jesuits had reported the Iroquois tribes doing a couple of centuries earlier.

Throughout the nineteenth century, eel continued to play a substantial role in the cuisine of the East Coast, and recipes for it were found in most of the cookbooks of the period. Fried, grilled, boiled, broiled, smoked, and stewed. Eel soup and eel stifle. Eel for breakfast, lunch, and dinner. Eels a-plenty, but after the Civil War some of the cookbook entries began to adopt a more defensive and cautious tone. The recipe for stewed eels in one of 1874's popular self-help books, *Common Sense in the Household,* by Marion Harland, managed to be both defensive and cautious. It began, "Inquire, before buying, where they were caught, and give so decided a preference to country eels as to refuse those fattened upon the offal of city wharves," and concluded: "The appearance and odor of this stew are so pleasing as often to overcome the prejudices of those who 'Wouldn't touch an eel for the world! They look so like snakes!'"

In 1884, the U.S. Department of Fisheries released a report called *The Fisheries and Fishery Industries of the United States,* compiled and written by George Brown Goode, which reviewed the nation's individual fisheries and their economic importance. The report's statistics were preceded by a long section called "Natural History of Aquatic Animals," in which Goode devoted almost 30 pages to the eel's life cycle and the history of eel reproduction research. He also looked at fisheries state by state and recorded, for instance, that in Massachusetts, out of 28 species of fish taken commercially in 1880, the eel ranked sixteenth, with almost 400,000 pounds reported. A little over a century later, in 1989, that figure was down to 29,900 pounds, and less than a decade after that, in 1997, eel fishing had practically disappeared in the state, with its entire commercial landings reported at 304 pounds.

The eel followed such other Old World favorites as garlic into disrepute, although garlic's popularity recovered while the eel's has not. The only Americans who continued to eat eel after World War II, when they could afford anything else, were those who did so out of ethnic habit: Italian, Polish, and Irish people who continued eating as they had always eaten. Current books about North American eating habits frequently fail to mention eels at all. *The American Century Cookbook,* published in 1997, compiled 500 of North America's favorite recipes during the twentieth century, and there is no mention made of eels. That classic midcentury cookbook, *The Joy of Cooking,* has one eel recipe—poached. *The Settlement Cookbook,* another standard at millennium's end, also has only one, and it is for fried eels. Or take a lavishly designed coffee-table volume like *The American Heritage Cookbook and Illustrated History of American Eating and Drinking,* published in 1964. There's plenty in it about salmon, cod, and trout, even sections on catfish and flounder, to say nothing of instructions for two lobster dishes and four ways to cook clams, as well as a full half-dozen recipes for crabs—but not a single word about eels. Nor do eels fare better in *The Great American Seafood Cookbook,* published in 1988, which contains four catfish recipes and over a dozen for crabs, and even tells readers how to cook a dogfish, without ever mentioning eels.

"People don't want to fool around with eels anymore," said Herb Slavin, 70, as we stood in front of his Fulton Fish Market stall in Manhattan in the middle of the organized chaos of busy people and whizzing forklifts that is the market any morning of the workweek. "Even the young Italian girls don't want to cook them. When I first started working here, 58 years ago, Italians absolutely had to have eel on the Christmas table. In those days, around Christmas, we'd probably sell 50,000 pounds of eel. These days, we'll be lucky to sell 1,000 pounds."

The Fulton Fish Market, occupying two long blocks down by the East River near the southern tip of Manhattan, is the best spot in the United States to take the pulse of fish consumption. It is the largest fish market in the country, and has been in formal existence since 1833, although fish were being unloaded from boats and sold on this spot a couple of decades before that. These days, of course, the fish arrive in airplanes and refrigerated tractor-trailer loads. In 1998, annual sales at the market were reported as more than $800 million.

"I haven't seen a boat off-load here for at least 20 years," said Slavin, a short man with tufts of gray hair, wearing a flannel shirt. He had stubby, strong, dirty hands, in one of which was clutched a bunch of orders—pieces of paper with numbers scribbled on them —as he supervised the comings and goings of the men around him assembling the components of those orders, hauling crates packed with ice and fish of one sort or another across the floor by means of a curved steel hook with a wooden handle, a tool carried by one and all who worked at the fish market.

It was August 2000 when I talked to Herb Slavin, and there was not a live eel on the premises. The only call for eels he got during most of the year came from Chinese or French restaurateurs, and they wanted dead eels. The Chinese prepared them in a variety of ways, he said, and the French used them as the main ingredient in bouillabaisse. There had been a Slavin family stall at the Fulton Fish Market since 1928, and even in the early years most of the live eel sales were to the ethnic market—Italian, German, and Polish people. While these customers ate eel, occasionally, year round, the real eel rush came at Christmas, when it seemed as if every Italian in the city was at the market looking for *capitone* ("big head"), which is what southern Italians call them. *Capitone* is the traditional dish on Christmas Eve, the key component of a seven-fish dinner, the *pranza di Natale*. While some of the fishes used for the Christmas meal may have varied from year to year, eel was always part of it. When Herb Slavin went to work for his father, December meant that the Slavin's stall would be full of boxes of live eels stacked up to the ceiling. "My father used to send me down to Virginia and Maryland, and I'd buy eels in the fall, getting ready for the Christmas rush of Italians."

For most of the rest of the year, there was always some traffic in live eels at the market, and these were caught locally. The Raritan Bay, bordering the southern coast of Staten Island and the northern coast of New Jersey, supported a healthy eel fishery, which went on all year. In the warmer months, the eels were caught in pots. Initially, the pots were made of oak and weighted. Freshly dead horseshoe crabs or soft clams were the preferred bait. When hard winter set in and the eels settled, dormant, in the mud, they were speared through the ice, and an experienced fisherman, who had a good touch with a spear, could catch as many as 70 pounds an hour, according to Clyde McKenzie in his book *The Fisheries of Raritan Bay*. Before 1900, eels were sent to the Fulton Fish Market daily on boats under sail, and then on motorized vessels.

The Hudson River's eels have long been prized for their rich flavor. In his *Letters from an American Farmer*, published in 1782, J. Hector St. John de Crèvecoeur, a French settler in the Hudson Valley, wrote about the preparations for winter: "Each family smokes fully one-half of the meat, fish, eels; in short everything we intend to preserve." People continued to fish for eels in the Hudson straight through the twentieth century, until 1976, when New York state prohibited all commercial fishing on the Hudson, including the eel fishery, because of high levels of PCBs in fish caught there. General Electric had been polluting the river with the chemical since the 1930s. People were advised not to eat any fish from the river, much less bottom-dwellers, on a regular basis. The publicity only accelerated the slide of eels on the slippery slope of consumer choice. The ban added to a public perception of the fish as a slimy mud-dweller, unfit for human consumption. Unfortunately, as more and more rivers fell victims to the pollutants from bankside industries, some reason began to be attached to this prejudice.

As early as 1900, dams and pollution from factories had greatly reduced the habitable space in many rivers for eels. There was an increasing number of dams too big for them to scale or go around. Numerous stretches of large rivers became unlivable due to the effluent and discharge of factories along their course. In 1884, George Brown Goode wrote about the Merrimac River, the eels of which Thoreau had written about some 35 years before. Its waters were already seriously degraded by the time Goode wrote, although in the early days before factories appeared on the river's banks, it supported a substantial commercial eel fishery. "Even the present generation recall the time when the river was well stocked with fish," Goode reported. "William Stark, esq., at the Manchester centennial celebration held October 22, 1851, says: 'My father has seen the shad so thick as to crowd each other in their passage up the falls to gain the smooth water above, so that you could not put your hand in without touching some of them, and yet there were more alewives than shad, and more eels than both.'"

Conditions have gotten worse since Goode's time, of course. The big, red brick factories of the late nineteenth century have been silent, crumbling for decades, but water quality has continued to decline. The eel, even with its amazing adaptive capacity to thrive in both salt and fresh water, seems to be quite sensitive to pollution. Certainly, as a bottom-dweller, it is highly vulnerable to the ill effects of bioaccumulation, the process by which toxic substances build up in an animal's body. There is fairly widespread scientific agreement that the eel is slow to detoxify, to rid itself of things like organochlorine pesticides and PCBs. In fact, some experimental evidence suggests that an eel may never be able to detoxify itself. This does not bode well for eels, but it might carry some benefits for humans. A number of marine biologists have suggested that the eel could provide us with a good biomonitor of pollution, that an analysis of toxic substances in its tissues will give a reliable reading on the quantity of such substances in the sediment at the bottom of a body of fresh water.

Canada's Saint Lawrence River has long supported an eel fishery, which primarily captures silver eels as they make their way back downriver, bound for the Atlantic and the Sargasso. Half a million may be caught each year. Eelers have been warning for years that the numbers of young eels going upriver are way down, and a counter installed at an eel ladder by a dam on the Saint Lawrence revealed that the number of juveniles was, in fact, down drastically.

Elvers, apparently, were hardly entering the river. Since an eel is likely to spend anywhere from 7 to 16 years upriver before descending toward the eelers' pots, it takes a long time for a collapsing elver recruitment to have an impact on a silver eel fishery, but in another few years some scientists predict that eels, and their fishery, will have virtually disappeared from the Saint Lawrence.

A number of theories have been put forward to explain why elvers are not choosing to come up the river. Some say it may be a change in the current patterns of the Atlantic or simply part of a cyclical rise and fall in recruitment. But many point to the well-documented presence of heavy metals and organochlorines in the sediment of the upper Saint Lawrence and Lake Ontario, the places to which the juvenile eels migrate to develop into adult females. It is one of North America's most industrialized drainage basins, and one of its most contaminated. The sediments of these waters are rich in heavy metals like mercury, lead, and cadmium, all stewed in a broth of organochlorine pesticides and herbicides, and PCBs.

The decline in juvenile recruitment may be nothing more than Martie Bouw's Waffle House theory in action: just as Marie Bouw will not go in a place that she perceives as unclean, so the eel swims on, past the mouth of the chemical sewer system that was once the mighty Saint Lawrence River. Eels are extremely sensitive animals and choose to avoid contaminated areas. Those that arrived before things reached their present excessively polluted state will live out their lives and come back downriver, although researchers have found an unusually high number of vertebral malformations and liver lesions in recent years among silver eels descending the Saint Lawrence. With their exceptionally keen olfactory senses, glass eels may simply refuse to enter a highly contaminated river.

An eel has four nasal cavities instead of the usual two, a pair for respiratory function located just below the eyes, and a pair above its mouth, where fish normally have them. The eel takes in water here and expels it from the posterior nostrils. The extra nasal cavities are believed to be entirely dedicated to smelling. In his classic reference work, *The Eel,* Friedrich-Wilhelm Tesch writes: "The eel is thus almost as sensitive to smell as the dog, which is not surpassed by any other animal." One of the eel's favorite foods is the tubiculous bloodworm. Tesch found that an eel could still smell five bloodworms that were ground fine and mixed with 667 million liters of water.

"You can take one liter of a certain type of alcohol, pour it into the Great Lakes, and an eel will smell it," said Uwe Kils, a 48-year-old German oceanographer at the Rutgers Institute of Marine and Coastal Sciences field station at Little Egg Harbor on the New Jersey coast. "The Great Lakes compose about 19 trillion liters, so you are talking about being able to smell something at one part per 19 trillion. That's a very acute sense of smell."

How does one determine when an eel can, or cannot, smell something? Simple, said Kils. Put an electrode in the part of its brain that reacts to smell and dilute until there is no measurable response. "The eels probably have the best nose on the planet. They suck water in constantly, through the two nasal tubes at the front of their heads, and the nose is lined with thousands of cells."

Kils, who came from northern Germany near the border with Denmark, was quick to say he felt more Danish than German. He looked a northern type: tall, ruddy-faced, blond, blue-eyed. He had spent a lot of time studying eels, although his specialty was krill, the small, shrimplike crustaceans in the Arctic Ocean on which whales feed. He was among the scientists who believed that eels had the potential to be excellent environmental monitors, and environmental monitoring was Kils's particular passion. One of his pet projects at Rutgers envisioned putting a data collector at the end of a miles long, underwater fiber-optic cable in the ocean, constantly analyzing the water quality and posting the results on the Web. He was certain that if given an opportunity to do so, people would monitor the conditions of their favorite bodies of water on a daily basis.

High-tech underwater equipment was another of Kils's areas of expertise. He initiated a project with students at a local vocational school in coastal New Jersey to design and build an eel ladder that would house a high-tech camera to film glass eels as they climbed it. "We got a few oaks that were cut down by the companies who are developing the Pine Barrens here, and, using old shipbuilding tools, we sliced the tree in two halves, hollowed it out, and put it back together to make a tube. On the inside, we put an old fishing net donated by fishermen and filled the inner parts with cutting-edge, fiber-optic stuff and a highly sophisticated magnifying eyepiece. The fiber optics illuminate the inside with light that's of a bandwidth the eels cannot see. For them it's dark, and we can observe the eels climbing up, and it's just amazing. They are outrageously beautiful. We can see them crystal clear on the monitors."

Kils has developed a system, using the same kind of setup, to put the eels to work as biomonitors. He explained it to me at his kitchen table, at one end of which was a small aquarium holding a thin, foot-long, four-year-old eel named Oscar, who while we sat talking either swam unceasingly up and down behind the glass, or was totally at rest, perched on its tail, absolutely still. To test for contamination, Kils used glass eels. He took samples of water from different streams and rivers and pumped them through a tube to see how the elvers reacted to them. In this manner, he postulated, water could be identified as contaminated and work could begin on identifying the pollutants and the polluters.

Another environmental use to which Kils believed eels could be put was controlling mosquitoes. The Pine Barrens of New Jersey, with its cranberry bogs and marshlands, has a tremendous mosquito problem, and Kils came up with an answer. An eel, he said, imprints on its first food in fresh water as its food of choice. If it is fed mosquitoes, it will subsequently hunt them out, and only when it cannot get enough mosquitoes to make a meal will it settle for something else.

"Eels start to eat at the transition from salt water to fresh water. That moment when they leave the salt water, they develop within two or three days the respiratory system and the gut and other stuff. They really change totally in two days. It's amazing to see. From leptocephalus to the wild stage with gills and a beating heart. It's one of the most magic things in marine life. Nobody knows how they do it. Then, they take their first bite."

Kils raised his pet eel, Oscar, along with many other glass eels, through that "magic thing," and he did it with mosquitoes. "We raised mosquitoes like crazy. It was difficult to raise so many mosquitoes to feed all those mosquito killers. Oscar was two-and-a-half years old before we could wean him away from mosquitoes. Before that, he would not eat anything but mosquitoes. They learn how to catch them and rip them apart. We got some beautiful video of how they turn them around and rip them apart."

He dropped a piece of honeyed ham in the aquarium, which Oscar tore at and worried into smaller pieces that he gulped down. "We wanted to advertise this as a natural mosquito control. We wanted to find a way to kill the mosquitoes that live in tide pools that are not connected to the ocean, and where eels and fish cannot get in. These are a real problem here. We raised hundreds of thousands of glass eels, put them on a plane, and dropped them out of the air into these ponds. Instead of spraying DDT, you can spray glass eels trained to eat mosquitoes. When we have taught them to be mosquito killers, they are very effective pest controllers.

"But, then, this all got political, and I had to leave that research. They are spraying from helicopters on us here. They fly over and spray. Mosquito control is a big, big business here. Many people work in it. They have dozens of helicopters and a lot of money."

He declined to explain the details of how the project came to be derailed. It was not the first, nor last, time that Uwe Kils's research would bring him into conflict with political interests. Germany, too, has environmental troubles that have been highlighted by contaminated eels. In a sampling of 494 eels from the Elbe River, captured and analyzed between 1979 and 1987, 42 percent of the eels had heavy metal contents exceeding the maximum permitted level. Kils complained of government and corporate interference with his research in both Germany and the United States. Never mind, he said; he didn't want to talk about the specifics of the battles. He had a lot of other ideas. On the Internet, he had created ecoscope.com/eelbase.htm—the Web's only eel server.

It was the news of the East Coast eel world: In the fall of 2000, Martie Bouw was driving his Volvo truck for Delaware Valley Seafood and Barry Kratchman. Holland Seafood was not in the business of buying and shipping eels that season. It was not a bad year to be drawing a paycheck and letting someone else take the risks. Barry told me over the phone that he was "staying busy," but the dollar was still way up, making it cheaper for Europeans to buy some of the abundance of product available from Europe's eel farms rather than American eels. The price being paid to eelers was down to around $1.35 a pound. I had called Barry Kratchman to ask him if this alliance with Martie was the big change in the eel business he had alluded to when we ate dinner in Philadelphia.

"Look, it's just like I told you then," he said, an edge of irritation coming across the phone line. "I don't want to talk about any of this yet. There are going to be some big changes in the eel business. It's something that's underway. I don't want it in a book. You know, this is a business where people don't like to talk much about what's actually going on. I wouldn't want to be reading about the *details* of my business in your book. Understand?"

Of course I understand. Anyone who has spent any time around eelers and eel dealers recognizes it instantly. The eeler's attitude of "I'm minding my own business, why aren't you?" makes the eel market as slippery a proposition to describe as an eel is to hold. From North Carolina to Maine, eelers and eel dealers keep their business to themselves, and they appreciate other people who do the same.

"My neighbors don't have any idea what I do, and that's how I like it," said Dick Hopkins, as he thumbed the button on a remote control to roll up his overhead double garage doors and reveal a half-dozen tanks bubbling in the shadows. They were gurgling, oxygenating, preparing to receive a ton of bait eels en route from Philadelphia in a Delaware Valley truck. Hopkins would take delivery of those eels and wholesale them to bait shops up and down the

New England coast. The garage was attached to a lovely, two-story shingled house set deep in the woods on a well-kept lot along the ragged coastline of Rhode Island.

"It's our whole life, this place," Hopkins told me, as we sat on his patio waiting for the truckload of eels. He was a big guy with close-cropped gray hair and a trimmed white mustache, his skin burnished by a lot of time outdoors. He had a big frame and a big face, with small blue eyes, and he was wearing a T-shirt and jeans. "My wife and I have put a lot of work into it."

Apart from Asian food markets, the last domestic market for U.S. eel dealers is made up of people who fish for striped bass and use eels for bait. For a number of years, the striped bass population along the eastern and northeastern U.S. coast was threatened, and in 1984 a moratorium on fishing for them went into effect. It was so successful in allowing the population to recover that in 1990 it was lifted. An eel, about nine inches long, three or four years old, is the most appetizing thing in the world to a striped bass, and Barry Kratchman told me that during the fishing season he sold some 5,000 pounds of bait eels a week, at about seven eels to the pound. Eelers have to sell to a dealer to get an adult eel to Europe, but getting the contents of the day's pots down to the bait shop at the local marina is a lot easier, and many eelers cull out the smaller bait eels and sell them directly. People fishing for stripers were buying eels from the bait shops for $1.35 each in the fall of 2000.

Fishing with a young eel as bait is not particularly pleasant. The generally practiced method of doing so is to grasp one with an old towel, hook it through its lips, and troll it along behind a boat, giving it a semblance of swimming along. It is best not to look in an eel's eyes as it is impaled. Nevertheless, a battle with a 30-pound striped bass can be sufficient inducement to overcome any reluctance to bait a hook, and during striper season a lot of young eels have their lives cut short in New England and the mid-Atlantic states.

"Striper fishermen can't catch their own bait; they need professionals to find it," said Hopkins. "Bait is what I do. I have a small live-haul truck. I buy bait eels and sell them. I started supplying that market at the same time as demand went up and supply went down. I've got bait shop owners up and down the East Coast; most of them take 20 to 30 pounds a week. I've showed them how to keep the eels alive and sell them as a bait, and I'm their supplier.

"The season is May to December. The customers at the bait shops are sport fishermen, and for them the season is over when their wives tell them it's time to go shopping for Christmas presents. Other than myself, there's nobody I know of making a living out of striper bait. The key is service. That's my business philosophy. You have to be able to keep the bait shops in eels."

To make sure he will be able to do that, he is taking delivery of about a ton of eels from Barry Kratchman and Delaware Valley Seafood. He will pay for them on delivery, so his mission over the next couple of weeks will be moving them from his garage to bait shops. "Nobody other than my customers knows what I do for a living. I don't advertise it, but I do work hard, 80 or 90 hours a week. I just bought a new truck six months ago, and I've already put 25,000 miles on it."

The eel truck pulled in about noon. A driver and his helper, aboard a small live-haul truck with eight tanks that made Martie's new rig look extremely spiffy indeed. The Delaware Valley truck was not rusty, but it was nowhere near new, either, and had seen a lot of eel-hauling miles. The driver parked the truck in front of the garage, and the eels were unloaded into plastic barrels through a big hose from the live tanks on the flatbed. The barrels were lifted onto a platform scale to be weighed, then lugged into the garage and dumped into the tanks. It took Hopkins and the driver's helper 45 minutes to unload them, while the driver waited. Hopkins wrote a check to Delaware Valley, and sent the truck on its way back to Philadelphia. He closed the garage doors and went into his house for lunch. Inside the garage, in the darkness, 2,000 eels swam ceaselessly to and fro, gauging the dimensions of their new confinement.

CHAPTER 6
Fishing and Farming

Dick Hopkins not only bought and sold eels, he fished for them, and had been doing so for 15 years. He set some 200 eel pots in the brackish estuaries and so-called salt ponds behind the barrier beaches up and down the Rhode Island coast. The state's coastline has about 20 miles of these salt ponds. They are fed by little brooks and fresh water on the one hand, and the Atlantic on the other. Hopkins had fished them all at one time or another. He set his pots only a few feet deep and did not mark them with buoys, but rather went along with a big hook and grappled for his lines on the bottom to locate them. "I don't want anyone to be able to find my pots and rob them," he told me. "People are probably better to each other down there in North Carolina, but up here you can't trust anyone."

There are numerous commercial fishermen in Rhode Island, making a living from whatever they can fish at a given time of the year—lobsters, quahogs, fluke—but Hopkins is the only person in Rhode Island making a full-time living from eels. If it were not for the bait eel business he would not be able to do so. "I used to catch big quantities of adults, and did well at it for many years. I used to catch 1,000 pounds a day. Now, a good day might be 200 pounds. Fortunately, as the number of big eels declined, they opened up striper fishing, and the demand for bait eels grew."

All around Narragansett Bay, the oldest residents remember when there was decent money to be made from eels. They could be trapped in the summer and speared in the winter. An eel in winter is dormant, wrapped in mud, an easy target when the rivers have frozen over. People all over New England would take to the ice to spear eels. Many a fisherman in Rhode Island and Connecticut augmented his income that way. In December 1876, the *Mystic Press* in Mystic, Connecticut, noted: "The eelers appeared on the river last week after a long absence, and the lovers of eel 'smudder' may now gratify their gustatory longings for that savory potpourri." A "smudder" was, apparently, a smother, a rich dish made with a crust. Yet another variety of eel pie.

"I knew a lot of guys that speared them in the winter, but I never had the knack," Albert Brooks told me. But he did have a knack for turning an eel into hard cash. While he was in high school in the early 1950s, Brooks and his brother set 50 pots in the Mystic River; after they collected their catch, they kept the eels alive in a wooden carboy, immersed in the river, drilled through with a lot of little holes.

When I met Brooks, he was 64 and lived in a mobile home at the back of a trailer park set high on a bluff facing the same Mystic River. I went to see him early one evening. Geese flew across the sky in a shadowy V as the sun set. A little plot of trimmed grass grew in front of the trailer, where a tall flagpole was planted, sporting an American flag. He and his brother used to lay their pots in the wide stretch of river we could see through the picture window in his trailer as we sat talking in the living room. The two of them would take as many as 300 eels a night from their pots and sell them in one of two ways. The first began with packing them in a barrel with a big chunk of ice. The next day, a truck would pick them up and carry them to the Fulton Fish Market, 135 miles to the south. For eels sold like this, the brothers were paid 18 cents a pound. However, when they sold directly to consumers, they could charge more. Their customers were primarily Poles and Italians from the Mystic area. They would come to the Brookses' house and ask for, say, three pounds of eels. Albert would row out to where the carboy was anchored and get the eels, kill them, and clean them for the customer.

"We sold three pounds for a dollar, and there were three eels in a pound. So to sell a dollar's worth, I had to skin nine eels. We'd put them in a galvanized garbage can half full of water, to which we'd pour in half a can of Prince Albert tobacco, then put a towel over the top to seal them in. You'd put the tobacco in and they'd quiver and just go stiff. We'd wait fifteen minutes and take them out and skin them."

Someone with a live eel on hand may want to remember this technique for killing it, instead of using the most common one, which is simply to bash its head with a blow to the skull. Some sources, like *The Angler's Cookbook,* recommend pouring a large pot of scalding water over it. Others call for salt, and plenty of it. Put an eel in a deep bucket, or tub, they advise, and cover it with salt. The eel will react to the salt by releasing large quantities of slime and will be unable to breathe. It can take an hour or two before the eel is completely dead. Once it is dead, it is washed with cold water, which also rinses off the slime. A variation on this method is to just sprinkle the eels with salt, cover them with water, and let them soak for three or four hours. Those who prefer to anesthetize the eels first, let them set a brief spell in the freezer, which knocks them out, and then give them the salt treatment.

Albert Brooks had seen all these methods used. "In my parents' time, all the guys fished for eel. Before the Depression, and during it, all the poor people did. Used to be some real nice big eels up here. Since the 1960s, nobody's caught enough to make it pay. When I was a kid, all the poor people lived on the water, and now it's the rich people," he said, gesturing out the trailer home's picture window with its view across a lovely, broad reach of the Mystic River. On the far bank, huge white houses stood on manicured grounds that sloped down to the water. "In those days, no rich person would live by the water."

There are only so many ways to catch an eel, and while materials vary, the same methods have been used over centuries and millennia. Dwellers by the world's watersides have been catching eels since they have been eating fish. In 1636, a French missionary among the Canadian tribes reported:

> Eel in the proper season is an invaluable article to our Montagnais. I have admired the extreme abundance of this fish in some of the rivers of our Canada, where every year unaccountable hundreds are caught. They come just in time, for, were it not for this succor, one would be greatly embarrassed, more especially in some months of the year; the savages and the members of our orders use them as meat sent by Heaven for their relief and solace.
>
> They catch them in two ways: with a wicker basket, or with a harpoon during night by the light of fire. They construct with some ingenuity wicker baskets, long and wide, and large enough to hold five or six eels. When the sea is low, they deposit them on the sand in a suitable remote place, securing them in a manner that the tide cannot carry them off. At both sides they heap up stones, which extend like a chain or small wall on both sides, in order that the fish, which always seeks the bottom in encountering this obstacle, may glide slowly toward the aperture of the basket to which the stones lead.

The idea of using structure to guide eels into traps is an ancient one. Such a construction is called a weir, and if the missionaries had known anything about eel fishing, they would have known that the same methods were being used in the southern part of their home country, down around the Loire River, for instance. There are remains of eel weirs on the River Bann in Northern Ireland, that date back to 1,000 B.C., and today one of the world's most productive weirs is on that same river at Toomebridge, bringing the Lough Neagh Fishermen's Cooperative some 150 tons of silver eels a year. Weirs were also used on the fens in the waterlands of East Anglia, in southeastern England. As early as the Norman Conquest in 1066, eel rents were being paid from the fens, and the annual rents on some weirs came to many thousands of eels, according to *Food and Drink in Britain,* by C. Anne Wilson.

As for the wicker baskets, they, too, were being used around the world to trap eels at the same time the missionaries saw them in Canada. The oldest eel traps were made from reeds gathered in the wild. Certain plants gave a fibrous, strong reed that could be woven into a basket. The first one, no doubt, had the same basic design as every eel pot, eel trap, and eel box to follow: a funnel leading into a chamber from which the fish could not figure out how to return. If the traps are placed at the narrow end of a weir, there is no need even to bait them. If they are submerged in a river or estuary, they will have bait. Certainly prehistoric, and most probably primordial, eel trapping is a very old way to fish. Primitive weirs were followed by a wide variety of traps and nets designed to catch eels.

The most ancient of all fish baits is nothing. It is not easy to catch an eel with your hands, but practice and hunger can improve a person's success rate, and it is easier to trap an eel in the mud with a pair of hands than it is to manually capture most fish. As Tisquantum trod up eels from the Plymouth mud, we can be sure, people have been doing similarly almost as long as there have been human beings and rivers. Academics tend to divide all fishing into two categories: active and passive. Fish traps and weirs would fall into the passive category. The first active means of eel fishing was undoubtedly the stoop-and-grab, just as surely as the next oldest was spearing, practiced whenever an eel was likely to be laid up in the mud, which would be during the day in warm months and at all times during winter, when they could be speared through the ice.

Horace Beck, in *The Folklore of Maine,* described that state's winter eel fishery during the nineteenth century:

> Since the Mainites never lost their love of eels, men, warmly clad and armed with an ax and a multi-pronged spear on a long pole, would venture out on the brackish ponds and shallow salt water

bays to spend long hours chopping holes and probing the mud with their spears for eels. A wiggle at the end of the pole would indicate the quarry had been struck and it would then be hauled out and disengaged from the spear with a sudden shake. The eel would squirm a moment before freezing into a mass as solid as an old stick, and much resembling one. Later, in the warmth of the kitchen, they would thaw and often begin squirming again until dressed and ready for the pot wherein they would be stewed, boiled, baked, roasted or fried.

In most cases, the real art to spearing eels was not so much in the handling of the spear as in knowing an eel's habits and choice of habitat; supplied with that knowledge, one could just thrust a spear into the mud at more or less the right spot until an eel was found. Eel spears are designed differently around the world, but they are all variations on a basic trident. In Europe, where eel spears dating back at least 2,000 years have been found, their design developed into an eel comb, a kind of rake that was dragged through the mud, a giant comb with metal teeth that pierce and hold an eel. Eel combs are still used in Europe, and they were also being dragged across the bottoms of northern Connecticut rivers and bays as recently as 20 years ago, according to Albert Brooks.

One of the oddest ways to fish for eels was described by the Greek naturalist Oppian, who is thought to have written around 170 A.D., in Book XIV of his *Halieuticks of the Nature of Fishes*. The eeler obtains the long intestine of a fat, freshly slaughtered sheep and insets a reed into it, then lowers it into the water. The eel bites it and cannot dislodge its teeth. Its efforts alert the fisherman, who must then blow down the reed with all his might. "And so the air descends into the Eel," wrote Oppian, "fills its head, fills its windpipe, and stops the creature's breathing. And, as the Eel can neither breathe nor detach its teeth which are fixed in the intestine, it is suffocated and is drawn up. . . . Now this is a daily occurrence, and many are the Eels caught by many a fisherman."

More modern and conventional ways to catch eels include a

baited hook. Although earthworms are not part of their normal diet, eels share with other fish a frequently fatal passion for them. This fact is noted in the original how-to fishing guide in English, an essay in *The Book of St. Albans* published in 1496. As the first advice for the would-be angler in English, it marked the beginning of a genre that would eventually contain thousands of titles. While most of them would be written by men, this late medieval work is attributed to a woman, Dame Juliana Berners. It was so popular that ten editions were published within four years. Dame Juliana titled her contribution *A Treatyse of Fysshynge with an Angle.* She was no great fan of eels, as evidenced by the brief section she devoted to them: "The eel is an unhealthy fish, a ravener and devourer of fish's broods, and as for the pike, he is also a devourer of fish. I rate these below all others to angle. You will find the eel in holes at the bottom of the water, and he is blue-black. Sink your hook until it is within a foot of the hole, and your bait must be a large earthworm or minnow."

Perhaps the best-known of the English how-to-fish books is Izaak Walton's *The Compleat Angler,* originally published in 1653. Walton, in contrast to his predecessor, considered the eel well worthy of angling, and he devoted an entire chapter of his book to recounting the mysteries of an eel's reproductive habits. He seconded Dame Juliana's advice about earthworms and minnows, but added that there were plenty of other things that would do if these were not to hand, including chicken and fish guts. As to the technique for catching the eel, he wrote: "Put in your bait, but leasurely, and as far as you may conveniently: and it is scarce to be doubted, but that if there be an Eel within the sight of it, the Eel will bite instantly, and as certainly gorge it: and you need not doubt to have him if you pull him not out of the hole too quickly, but pull him out by degrees, for he lying folded double in his hole, will with the help of his tail break all, unless you give him time to be wearied with pulling, and so get him out by degrees, not pulling too hard."

Correct. If an eel can get its tail dug in somewhere, or wrapped around something, it can be virtually impossible to dislodge it. An eel's first reaction on noting that it is hooked is to find something on the bottom to wrap its tail around. Most of the time, once an eel has a grip, the outcome will be a broken line.

One of the oldest and most curious methods of handline fishing for eels does not use a hook. In Germany it is called *naring,* and in England it is known as bobbing. The first reference to bobbing for eels in the *Oxford English Dictionary* is from 1660. Bobbing involves taking from 20 to 80 large earthworms and passing a woolen thread through them with a big needle. This whole hank of worms and thread is then fished just above the bottom of a stream at the end of a length of line tied onto a stout pole. When an eel bites the worms, its short teeth become entangled in the thread long enough for it to be pulled up. On occasion, more than one eel at a time can be caught by bobbing.

A lot more people fish for eel in the United Kingdom than in the United States. In England, there are eel angler's clubs, members of which dedicate their free time to fishing for big eels. They keep extensive records on big eel catches—with a "big eel" defined as one weighing more than four pounds. Records fall slowly. On July 29, 1922, a record was set by an 8-pound, 8-ounce eel caught in a Bristol lake. Forty-seven years later, on the same date in 1969, an eel of 8 pounds, 10 ounces, was caught in a different Bristol lake. And then, in 1982, an eel weighing over 18 pounds was caught. Brian Crawford, in his 1983 book, *Fishing for Big Eels,* summed it up on behalf of his fellow amateur enthusiasts: "Pound for pound, ounce for ounce, the eel excels as a fighting fish."

In the United States, for people fishing bait from boat or bank, the problem is not how to catch an eel, but how *not* to catch one. These are people who would never consider eating an eel and for whom trying to get one off a hook represents a loss of valuable fishing time. For them, there is nothing quite so disappointing as to experience the excitement of having a float sink suddenly below the surface only to reel in the line and find that the something struggling on the other end turns out to be an eel.

"Man, it's good luck that put you on my bus today, because there's a question about eels I'm dying to know the answer to, and that's how to keep them from biting my bait," said the middle-aged, stout, dark-skinned man, who told me he had already worked 30 years for a security company, retired, and found out his pension had not been enough to meet the expenses of his family. He went back to work as a shuttle bus driver for the U.S. Department of Agriculture in Beltsville, Maryland.

Want to use the Ag Department's library? Get on the train. Bring a book. It's a good 45 minutes by rail outside Washington, way out in the green countryside at the last stop on the commuter train route. When you get there, walk outside and after a while a shuttle bus will come along and offer you a 15-minute ride to the library. The bus driver said he liked to spend his weekends out on his boat, fishing for spot and croaker in the Chesapeake Bay, and that an eel was not what he wanted to find on his line. "I can almost always tell when it's an eel. Most of the time, if I get a bite and say it's an eel, I'm not wrong. They don't take the line side to side like a fish, they go back, straight back every time."

Unlike with most other fish, the hard part of fishing for eels does not begin until after the eel has been landed. It is as sporting to catch as any other fish, because it pulls hard and puts up a good battle. But only after getting it out of the water do the angler's real problems begin. The prospect of having to handle a slimy eel, twisting and twining itself around a fishing line like ivy climbing up a pole, is not a pleasant one. What frequently happens is that after a few minutes of trying to hold the eel still enough to extract the hook, people just decide to sacrifice their tackle and end up cutting both hook and eel off their line, perhaps helping the fish, writhing on the ground with the hook in its mouth, back into the water with a push from a boot. For those who are unfamiliar with how to apply the three-fingered grip, getting hold of an eel long enough to get a hook out of its mouth does not qualify as quality fishing time. As an aid, a towel is good, any piece of rough-napped material that can give a hand a grip, but the oft-chosen newspaper is so insubstantial that it ends up in slimy wet shreds all over the place; and trying to hold an eel with a smooth cloth is about as easy as holding a handful of water.

There were centuries in the history of the United States when an eel qualified as something for an angler to bring home with a smile and expectations of a tasty meal. These days, folks would just as soon catch a cold as catch an eel. This, in a nation that supports a $450 million-a-year industry farming catfish, a fish every bit as much a bottom-dweller as an eel. In Europe, it is just the opposite. Farmed eel is an important component of European aquaculture, and it's a good day for the angler who catches a wild one. There is, however, absolutely no consumer interest in catfish, wild or farmed.

As the developed world exhausts the wild fish population, two things will happen. People will become more willing to buy what had previously been thought of as trash fish, and they will rely ever more heavily on aquaculture to put fish on their tables. Perhaps, as more prized species are reduced in number to the point that they virtually disappear from the U.S. market, North Americans will again come to include eel among the possibilities of what's for dinner. And, the neutral-flavored and nutritious meat of the catfish may one day grace European tables. Even if consumer tastes stay as they are, and these things do not come to pass, both catfish and eels are already playing important roles in aquaculture.

Fish farming is never easy, regardless of the species being grown. There is much more to it than just tossing a bunch of tiny fish into some water, taking them out again when they are big enough to sell, and keeping them fed between times. As on any farm, there are multitudinous things that can go wrong in trying to maintain optimum conditions for a fish's healthy growth. Farmers must be ever vigilant against diseases, of which there are many to which fish are susceptible and some that can wipe out an entire population. In addition, water quality is critical and can change rapidly. An eel farmer has these things to worry about, and a couple of other very tricky things particular to farming eels. Eel is the only fish being farmed that will not reproduce in captivity, so farmers are dependent on wild elvers to provide brood stock.

Another problem connected to the fact that all farmed eels come from the wild is that the food an eel usually needs to thrive is whatever it first learned to eat as an elver, and that first food is almost always alive. Despite their reputations as scavengers, eels are basically extremely picky eaters. A hungry eel will eat something dead if it needs to do so for survival, and it will eat plant matter as well, but the great bulk of an eel's diet in the wild consists of living animals smaller than itself. For those who set out to raise eels on a commercial basis, it is impossibly expensive to keep them supplied with live food. Aquaculture is based on the farmed fish adapting itself to a manufactured feed that can be purchased in bulk and relatively cheaply. Rather than eat standard aquaculture feed and thrive, however, a young eel will sometimes starve to death and will frequently eat only enough to keep itself alive, certainly not enough to speed it on toward a marketable size.

"Eels are a royal pain," said Margie Gallagher, who has spent a good deal of her professional life researching what an eel needs for an optimum diet and how to meet those requirements on a fish farm. "With eels, you're basically getting wild eels to begin with, and you're going to wind up throwing away about half of them, because 20 percent of them are never going to learn how to eat and they're going to starve to death or, more likely, their siblings are going to eat them. Then, there'll be some that eat but they just don't grow very well, and you're never going to be able to sell them."

On the fall day when I met her in her office, Gallagher looked more like a student than a professor of biology at East Carolina University's Institute for Coastal and Marine Resources. She was dressed in overalls and sandals, and she had long, auburn hair. She was born and raised in a Tennessee town so small that she had never been to a restaurant before she left home for the University of Tennessee. She earned her Ph.D. at the University of California and has been at East Carolina University researching fish nutrition since 1980. "I came here to raise eels. Originally all my work was with crustaceans, and after I got here it took me a while to get comfortable with eels. It was a year before I didn't mind touching them. People were just starting to get into farming them in this state. Basically, when something went wrong, we didn't have enough expertise in North Carolina to help.

"Eel farming just didn't work out here because of basically two reasons—disease and marketing. We were making progress on diseases, but not fast enough for people who had big investments in growing eels. The second was that lots of people just got put off by having to depend on the European market to buy their product. It wasn't as if they could just truck them to South Carolina, if they couldn't sell them here. Europe was the only market.

"I was really interested in developing a pelleted, dry diet. The Japanese had been raising eels for a hundred years on wet, moist diets. We showed that you could get them to eat pellets. You still had to train them initially to eat a wet diet, but as you do that, you mix in the dry and keep adding more and more of it, and by the time you're finished they're eating pellets—tiny little pellets, but they're dry.

"There were a lot of things we didn't understand. The Japanese, for instance, routinely separate out their eels; they size and separate them, size and separate them, size and separate them. Those that are not thriving get culled out. They use different net sizes. We weren't doing that. It takes a lot of time, but to the Japanese it's well worth it because they don't waste their time feeding animals that aren't going to grow."

When you're talking about eel consumption, one country stands out over all—Japan. It is fair to say that the Japanese value eels far more than do people of other cultures. To begin with, there are the quantities they eat and the money they spend doing so. In 1995, the Japanese consumed about 190 million pounds of eel, worth about $1.8 billion. Consumption had risen 22 percent over the preceding ten years. Eels have an importance in Japanese culture bordering on totemic.

The journey taken by eels to reach Japan is remarkably similar to that undertaken by U.S. and European species, and its life cycle seems to mirror theirs. The Japanese eel, *Anguilla japonica,* looks just like its Occidental cousins, although its vertebrae count differs slightly, and it is genetically distinct. Japanese eels are thought to be born as larvae in the great depths of the Pacific Ocean, about 1,200 miles south of Japan and the same distance east of the Philippines, in an area called the Ryuku Trench. Here, the Kuroshio current acts like the Gulf Stream in the Atlantic, and brings the leptocephali northwest to Japan. There is a trough of warm water on the southern edge of the Kuroshio current, much the same as exists in the Sargasso. Japanese eels are found from Korea to Hong Kong. It takes *japonica* elvers about a year to find fresh water in Japan, the same amount of time required by the American eel. The Japanese, however, say one thing distinguishes *japonica* from both American and European eels: taste. They much prefer to eat their own, claiming they are a fatter, tastier species. Just like everywhere else in the world, however, catch numbers in Japan are declining. In 1926, Japanese eelers caught about 8 million pounds of *Anguilla japonica,* according to Léon Bertin. In 1995, that figure was down to just under 2 million pounds, as reported by the Commercial Division of the U.S. embassy in Japan.

Eels are considered to be, absolutely, the food of choice during hot weather. Ordinarily, in Japan, Ox Day is the hottest of the year. The exact date on which it falls varies from year to year, but it will always be during a two-week period toward the end of July. During that time, people eat as much eel as they can, convinced that it imparts energy and stamina that help a person withstand the extremely hot and muggy conditions of a typical Japanese summer. The sale of eel skyrockets. The tradition of eel and Ox Day is said to date from the nineteenth century, when a famous samurai was quoted as saying that eating eel during hot weather gave him extra energy.

Even when the weather is not hot, the Japanese eat a lot of eel, which they call *unagi* when it is taken during its freshwater phase and *anago* when it is captured in salt water. The most common way they eat it is as *kabayaki,* prepared in a process that essentially consists of skewering it, quickly steaming it, then dipping it in a slightly sweet, soy-based sauce and grilling it. The Japanese have been processing eel this way since the 1600s. Nowadays, *kabayaki* is often vacuum-packed and shipped to sushi restaurants around the world to make eel sushi, a ubiquitous dish on the menus of Japanese restaurants. Numerous other Japanese eel dishes include the popular *unadon* (fresh eel grilled on skewers and served over rice), eel liver soup, and eel bones deep fried until they are crisp, then eaten as a snack. Nor do the Japanese disdain elvers, called *dojo,* which they prepare in a kind of omelet, not unlike the way people around the mouth of England's Severn River prepare their elver omelets.

Between 1990 and 2000, the per capita consumption of eel rose steadily in Japan, while the numbers of eel caught in the wild went down. The amount of processed eel eaten by Japanese consumers more than quadrupled, from 24.2 million pounds in 1986 to over 100 million in 1996. Most of that demand has been filled by farmed eel.

The first modern eel farms in Japan date back to 1894, so the Japanese have been at it for a long time. As catches fell in the wild, aquacultural production mounted. Intensive farming methods have reduced the normal 18-month, grow-out cycle to 12 months. However, despite increased amounts of time and money spent on research, farmers in 2001 were still completely dependent on elvers from the wild. In 1974, two Japanese biologists succeeded in artificially fertilizing eel eggs, amid widespread optimism that aquacultured leptocephali were about to become a reality. By injecting mature male and female eels with hormones, the biologists were able to induce sexual maturation. The females developed eggs, which the scientists harvested and fertilized with male milt. Within two days, larvae began to hatch out. It looked as if one of nature's oldest riddles had been solved. Not so fast: after five days, all of the newly hatched larvae were dead.

Curiously, even though they were obviously failing to get all the nourishment they required, the larvae did grow, and in five days had increased in size from 4.8 to 6.2 millimeters. In the efforts that have followed since 1974, artificially hatched larvae have been kept alive for as long as 25 days, and they do grow during that time.

No one knows what, or even *how* a leptocephalus eats. Scientists are not sure whether leptocephali actually feed on tiny matter that gets digested in their primitive guts, or they take in nourishment through the skin during the long drift in open ocean. All that is certain is that they must take in nourishment in some form, because they do grow. Johannes Schmidt's larval collections in the first quarter of the twentieth century turned up larvae ranging from 7 millimeters to 84 millimeters (0.3–3.3 inches) in length at the northern end of the larva's journey. The real challenge of getting eels to reproduce in captivity is not obtaining leptocephali, because these can now be produced artificially, but in nourishing a larva, keeping it alive and growing until it reaches the 65 millimeters or so (about two and a half inches) it will need to begin its transformation into an elver searching for fresh water. The conditions in which leptocephali spend that first part of their lives are not easy to mimic.

The question of how to keep leptocephali alive has much more than solely theoretical importance for the Japanese. In the late 1980s, the annual recruitment of *Anguilla japonica* elvers fell off drastically, which meant a shortage in elvers for the farms and, within a few years, a shortage of farm-raised adults on the market. The price for *japonica* elvers rose to the equivalent of $2,500 a pound during 1997. With the market for adult eels moving some $2 billion worth a year, the shortage of elvers for Japan's farms had worldwide repercussions.

One of those was gunplay on the banks of New Jersey's creeks and rivers. When the Japanese could not get enough *japonica* elvers, they settled for elvers from Europe and America. And that is when people in New Jersey from all walks of life, high school teachers to pipe fitters, took up fishing for elvers on dark nights when the tide was coming in. These newly minted eelers had their favorite spots and were prepared to defend them with pistols. The price for glass eels rose until it reached $500 a pound at the riverbank. The boom lasted for two years, 1996 and 1997, before New Jersey, like North Carolina before it, made elver fishing illegal. Asian eel dealers were not the only ones buying up elvers. Barry Kratchman had no trouble finding customers for every pound of elvers he could buy. "I'd put $40,000 in cash in my pants pocket and drive from Philadelphia to Cape May, New Jersey, at 2:00 in the morning," he remembered. "It was crazy, a nightmare. We were making some money, but I was glad they made it illegal."

It was just as well that they did. For no discernible reason, and flying in the face of gloomy predictions from most scientists, the 1998 run of *Anguilla japonica* picked up again, and by the end of 1999 the riverbank price for elvers in New Jersey was down to about $15 a pound, if someone could be found to buy them. The Japanese are quite definite about their tastes in live eels. If they can't get Japanese eel, which is always their first choice, they will settle for European, but only if neither of those is available, will they eat American. Consequently, the market for European elvers has stayed stronger, because the Chinese buy them to raise for the Japanese market.

However, American eel can be used to make *kabayaki,* and the Chinese have invested tremendous amounts of money in eel farming operations to provide *kabayaki* to the Japanese. In 1999, there were 67 *kabayaki* processing plants in China, each with the capacity to produce 3,000–4,000 tons a year. The Chinese eel farms are always in the market for elvers from the Oria in Spain, the Loire in France, or the Severn in England. New European legislation prohibiting the export of elvers, combined with the restrictions recently imposed on the fishery in the United States, will likely leave the Chinese with a big elver deficit.

One of the few people who is prepared to take advantage of that situation, should it arise, is Willy Bokelaar, Martie Bouw's expartner at Holland Seafoods. He was raising American elvers in large tanks in a Virginia warehouse, bringing them along to fingerling size, then selling them to Chinese farms that grew them out to adults and turned them into *kabayaki.* At 41, Willy Bokelaar had been in the eel business for a long time. He was 16 when he got his first job, cleaning eels in the local market of the small Dutch town where he grew up.

"People in Holland only wanted live eels in those days," Bokelaar told me, sitting in the office at his warehouse near the coast of southern Virginia. He and his wife, Mirella, had a five-month-old son. Willy was bald in front, with dark brown hair and a trimmed mustache. With his wire-rimmed glasses, he looked more like a university professor than an eel farmer. "Cleaning eels is about the worst job you can imagine. Nobody does that anymore. It's a filthy, dirty job. All that's over with. Young married people today are both working, and they just want to come home and put something in the microwave."

Elver fishing is illegal in the state of Virginia, but Willy Bokelaar has a special elver permit, issued in an effort to encourage his aquaculture operation. At any given time in the constant twilight inside the warehouse, his 24 ever-gurgling fiberglass tanks hold about 3.5 million eels in various stages of growth. To grow an eel from an elver to a fingerling takes him about eight months. "I finished this place in 1998 and began operations in February 1999," Bokelaar said. "I wanted to do it in North Carolina, but the state would not give me any help. I decided a while ago to get out of adult eels. There's not much future in it. The price in Europe for wild eels hasn't changed in ten years. Fishermen can't make any money. Their costs are higher all the time, but they get paid the same. It's doomsday in the adult eel industry.

"Farming is the future. I hope to establish a grow-out industry here, make a finished product, take advantage of the U.S. market for *kabayaki* in Japanese restaurants here. They import a significant amount. The numbers are flabbergasting. I'd like to contract with local farmers around here to dig ponds, grow them out."

Bokelaar used a commercial aquaculture feed with a fish-meal base, controlled by a computer-driven system in which a feeding tray released measured sprays of fine feed as it glided back and forth over a tank. He had been feeding elvers for many years, and if anyone could get them to eat and thrive, he said, he could. "Most people can't believe the density levels here. One of our secrets is our circulation system. A lot of people sell systems that have problems. Ours is an extremely expensive system, but it does what it's supposed to do."

Longshan was the largest of the Chinese companies that Willy Bokelaar sold to, and the company had recently started an eel farm in Monaville, Texas, with two 45-acre ponds, in which they grew out American eels. The only other person trying to farm eels in the United States was a Florida farmer named Dugan Whiteside, and he never had much luck at it. There were just too many things that could go wrong. His record year for eels was a harvest of about 8,000 pounds in 1987. In 1990, the *Wall Street Journal* did a piece about his company, Anguilla Fish Farms, and called him "the emperor of eels." However, by the late 1990s, Whiteside had virtually stopped farming eels and was growing striped bass and tilapia instead. He always had a problem getting a sufficient number of juveniles to eat prepared feed, he told a magazine called *AgVentures* in 1999.

To turn a profit, eel farming in the Northern Hemisphere generally requires year-round access to warm, clean water, and that usually means an expensive recirculating system. Willy Bokelaar declined to put an exact price tag on his operation but said it was "much more" than a million dollars. Start-up costs in Europe are equally high, but at least the Europeans could grow the eel out knowing there was a local market for it. It might be up some years and down others, but it was a market. That was a big help. The total EU production of eels, farmed and wild, in 1997, was almost 18 million pounds, of which about 12.5 million pounds were consumed in the country where they were caught, with virtually all the rest being sold to other EU countries, according to a recent report on European aquaculture.

Of those 18 million total pounds, some 660,000 pounds were raised by Juan Torres, whose company, Valenciana de Acuicultura, has been raising eels since 1984 with a recirculating, warm water system in a large covered building just north of Valencia, Spain. His operation is one of the six largest eel farms in Europe using this advanced technology. Torres, 64, is a short, compact man, balding, his silver hair combed back. He has blue eyes and a sharp glance.

"People eat a lot of eel here in Valencia," he told me. "After that, I sell them all over Europe. We sell strictly in Europe. It's too much of a hassle to sell live eels to Asia; the logistics are a nightmare. But, my first market is always local."

In El Palmar, a few miles south of Valencia on the shores of the Albufera marshlands, eel is prepared as eel and pepper, *aal i pebre,* in Valenciano, the variant of Catalan — itself a minority language — spoken in the province of Valencia. People there eat a lot of eel. *Aal i pebre* is usually served as a first course and consists of small chunks of eel, stewed in a shallow clay pot with olive oil, garlic, paprika and thinly sliced potatoes until the eel is firm and the potatoes are tender. For many years, the Albufera supported a healthy eel fishery, and much of that product wound up as *aal i pebre* on local tables. As water quality declined in the Albufera, and catch numbers plummeted, Juan Torres stepped in to fill the market niche with his farm-raised product, and local consumption remained high in the year 2000, with about 60 percent coming from Valenciana de Acuicultura's tanks.

In the early 1980s, his father sold some farmland near Valencia, and Juan, who was working then as an industrial chemist, received some of the money from the sale. He wanted to invest in a business and became interested in aquaculture. After a lot of research, he assembled a group of investors and went into eel farming.

By December 2000, he had 130 tanks in a vast, well-lit warehouse near the beach at Puzol. Some eel farmers keep their eels in low lights, but Torres did not think it made any difference. Once the eels were more than a few inches long, he put them in tanks with an automatic feeding system. In each tank, they gathered beneath a metal rod that hung from a feed tray. Every time an eel nudged the rod, a tiny pellet of food the size of a small pebble fell off the tray toward the water. The eels gathered at the surface in a roiling, moiling dance, writhing bodies standing up out of the water, rising like cobras being charmed out of a basket. They gathered in a huge cluster around the rod, nudging, nudging, and nudging. When they were full, they swam away.

"Everything is computerized, from the water level in each tank to the records of how many eels are in each one and at what stage of growth they are," Juan Torres said, wonder in his voice as if he still found it amazing himself. "It's a very sophisticated program."

Seth Willis lived with his wife and children in a mobile home outside of Arapahoe, North Carolina. He fished for a living, one thing and another, depending on the season. He had crab pots, pound nets, gill nets, an oyster rake, and a lot of eel pots, and he spent most of his days on his boat. During eel season, he sold a lot of eels to Martie Bouw and was, geographically, Holland Seafood's closest supplier. His trailer sat on a piece of land belonging to his family, up the dirt road from the turn-off to Martie's place. There was a paved highway just the other side of the Willis place, and Seth's father, Lionel, who had gone to grade school with Billy and Lucille Truitt, owned a small grocery store about 50 yards on past where the dirt road entered the paved one, a real old-fashioned crossroads grocery store with a couple of gas pumps out front.

Lionel Willis's Grocery was about as far removed from most twenty-first-century places to buy food as Lucille Truitt's Ole Store was from a mall. The grocery's shelves held a sparse assortment of canned goods; a large, white enamel meat case, which was empty, sat in the middle of the floor; and near the front door was a cash register, but as often as not people would put whatever they bought on their bills, because why else buy at a crossroads store where the prices are higher? Next to the counter on which the register sat, by a plate-glass front window, were a stove and a few chairs with good views of the gas pumps and the road outside.

Both Willises, Seth and Lionel, were big men, built along the same lines as Billy Truitt—solid and substantial. Father and son got along well. A time or two during most days, Seth found a reason to drop by the store. If he wanted to ask or tell his father something, he was as likely to walk up from the trailer to do so as to use the phone. One afternoon, when I was in the grocery, the talk turned to eels and their long journey from and to the Sargasso Sea. That was when

Lionel Willis said the smartest thing I ever heard anyone say about the subject: "I know what all the scientists say about what they do, and the trip they make. It may be right but it ain't reasonable."

That's right. It ain't reasonable. In fact, that is what draws us to the eel, its life so opposite to our own, its slipperiness both literal and metaphorical—an elusive, unknowable fish that feeds at night, and is hard or impossible to hold or quantify or even observe. Few people who work with them remain unimpressed by eels; the sense of wonder they inspire only deepens over time for many of those who study them. Scientists wind up shaking their heads, perplexed, giving a self-deprecating kind of the-joke's-on-me chuckle when considering how little is definitively known about eels. Rutgers University's Uwe Kils laughed like that when he told me he believed eels were once inhabitants of Atlantis; and Margie Gallagher at East Carolina University laughed the same way when she said that the more she worked with eels, the more she was convinced that they were actually alien beings from another planet.

There is nothing so amazing in the piscine world as catadromous and anadromous species, those few kinds of fish that are able to live parts of their lives in both fresh and salt water, each of which demands distinct organic processes. It is as if humans were to drink fresh or salt water at different times in their lives. We appear to be governed by a monotonous and restricted life cycle compared to that of eels. We are born and die with one form that grows and ages, but remains basically the same, and one set of needs that nourish and drive us from cradle to grave, the breathing-eating-sleeping patterns of our lives, virtually unchanged from beginning to end. An eel, on the other hand, begins life as neither male nor female, transforms its body twice, changes the element in which it lives, and has a life that varies between periods of intense activity and virtual hibernation according to the season.

All these things we know, and yet we know next to nothing about eels. The task of understanding their habits remains immense, and their secrets appear likely to remain mysteries for some time. Such a common creature and still so hidden. An animal that naturally moves in darkness, that loves the warm wet of mud and happily passes its days resting there. With dark comes hunger, and the night-time search for food. Years later, in another shadowy realm, will come the long passage back to the Sargasso, the eel's piercing blue eyes grown wide for vision in the dim blue light of deep ocean. No more seasons of ravenous hunger or torpor in the mud. That has all ended, replaced by a long swim of many months' duration, cease-less moving in the grip of a directional pull far beyond human ken, ever closer to that special zone in the Sargasso. The sexually mature eels will burn their stored fat to reach the mating grounds, use up all their reserves to reach that place where they can reproduce and die, completing one of the most curious life cycles on this large and varied earth.

A
Taste
of
Eel

There are many countries with eels in their lakes, streams, and rivers, and the people who live in most of them have their favorite ways of preparing eels to eat. Maybe it is for the best that people in North America have virtually stopped consuming eels, sparing the remaining *Anguilla rostrata* population the ravages of being in demand on the U.S. market. If North Americans ate eels the way people in other parts of the world do, there would not be a wild eel left on the continent. Still and all, it does seem a shame to have lost such an old and tasty food from our national menu, and to have shunned the eel's mysterious presence in our lives. For those who would like to do their part in bringing an appreciation for the taste of eel back to North America, a few recipes and possibilities are presented below, beginning with a recipe that uses no eel, but is so tasty as to merit inclusion: Lucille Truitt's one-pot collard greens. Lucille says to fix them as follows:

Take a good-sized piece of lean baked ham, and let that cook in the pot while you wash the collards real good with two or three waters to get off the insecticides and the grit. Cut them up and add them to the meat with some salt and cook until the greens are done. Collards are better after the first frost; they

dard eel recipe.
astern Europe,
es people have
ch, for instance,
re than a dozen
nnaire de Cuisine,
ary published in
l recipes, every-
e all the ways that
rench eel dish re-
ipes, all variations
sted in this recipe

n red wine
net. Brown small
more butter. When
d fried crisp in

aised eel in Europe,
been great lovers of
also mostly smoked,
mselves on their eel
become the south-
find eels in the New
ad been. Italy, Spain,
raditional, regional eel

methods for preparing
dish of stewed eels has
May, who learned his
efore spending the rest
ish nobility, gave these

an hour, or until they're

're done, make cornmeal
d fine meal in a bowl with
er faucet until it's firm
lumplings and put them
n also add potatoes.

an eel. Among her few
lt otherwise, about the
or seeing it served, was
d dipped in milk and
fried in a lot of grease
just about anything
in the popular culi-
. It was not always
North Carolina eels
on the table. New
hich was built for
Bern was named
ye with oysters,"
ce's eighteenth-

take great
dry them,
Eels, with
m all over
n put in
ith Butter,
d Bake it,

Virtually no country in Europe is without a stan[d]
Anguilla anguilla are found throughout western and [e]
as well as in western Russia, and in all these pla[ce]
found numerous ways of preparing them. The Fren[ch]
enjoy them in a wide variety of dishes. There are m[o]
recipes for eel in Alexandre Dumas's *Grand Dicti[o]*
published in 1873. A French gastronomic diction[ary]
1936, *Larousse Gastronomique,* listed 45 different e[el]
thing from fricaseed eel to cold eel aspics. Despit[e]
eel has been cooked over the years, the classic F[rench]
mains a *matelote.* There are innumerable *matelote* rec[ipes]
on a theme, the basics of which are succinctly li[sted]
from *A Concise Encyclopedia of Gastronomy:*

> Clean, skin, and cut up eel, and stew gently i[n]
> and water with salt, garlic and garnish bouq[uet]
> onions in butter and add to fish with a little [?]
> thoroughly hot, pour over thin slices of bre[ad]
> butter; remove bouquet before serving.

The Dutch consume almost half the farm-r[aised]
mostly as smoked eel. Germans have always [?]
their *Aal* and consume great quantities of it, [?]
although the citizens of Hamburg pride the[mselves]
soup. Early German settlers in what woul[d]
ern United States were every bit as glad to [?]
World as the English settlers further north h[ad]
Yugoslavia, Bulgaria, and Rumania all have t[raditional]
recipes as well.

One of the most frequently encountered [?]
eels is stewing, though just what goes into a [?]
changed greatly over the centuries. Robert [?]
culinary skills in sixteenth-century Paris, b[ut]
of his professional life as a cook for Engl[ish]
directions for stewed eels:

Virtually no country in Europe is without a standard eel recipe. *Anguilla anguilla* are found throughout western and eastern Europe, as well as in western Russia, and in all these places people have found numerous ways of preparing them. The French, for instance, enjoy them in a wide variety of dishes. There are more than a dozen recipes for eel in Alexandre Dumas's *Grand Dictionnaire de Cuisine,* published in 1873. A French gastronomic dictionary published in 1936, *Larousse Gastronomique,* listed 45 different eel recipes, everything from fricaseed eel to cold eel aspics. Despite all the ways that eel has been cooked over the years, the classic French eel dish remains a *matelote.* There are innumerable *matelote* recipes, all variations on a theme, the basics of which are succinctly listed in this recipe from *A Concise Encyclopedia of Gastronomy:*

> Clean, skin, and cut up eel, and stew gently in red wine and water with salt, garlic and garnish bouquet. Brown small onions in butter and add to fish with a little more butter. When thoroughly hot, pour over thin slices of bread fried crisp in butter; remove bouquet before serving.

The Dutch consume almost half the farm-raised eel in Europe, mostly as smoked eel. Germans have always been great lovers of their *Aal* and consume great quantities of it, also mostly smoked, although the citizens of Hamburg pride themselves on their eel soup. Early German settlers in what would become the southern United States were every bit as glad to find eels in the New World as the English settlers further north had been. Italy, Spain, Yugoslavia, Bulgaria, and Rumania all have traditional, regional eel recipes as well.

One of the most frequently encountered methods for preparing eels is stewing, though just what goes into a dish of stewed eels has changed greatly over the centuries. Robert May, who learned his culinary skills in sixteenth-century Paris, before spending the rest of his professional life as a cook for English nobility, gave these directions for stewed eels:

cook quicker. Cook them for about an hour, or until they're tender.

About twenty minutes before they're done, make cornmeal dumplings. Mix up medium meal and fine meal in a bowl with a little salt, and put under the hot water faucet until it's firm enough to hold together. Shape your dumplings and put them in the pot on top of the greens. You can also add potatoes.

Lucille would rather eat a possum than an eel. Among her few down east Carolina contemporaries who felt otherwise, about the only way anyone could remember eating eel, or seeing it served, was fried: skinned, cut into two-inch chunks, and dipped in milk and egg, then covered with cornmeal or flour and fried in a lot of grease or oil. Of course, Southerners are liable to fry just about anything in that fashion, but fish, in particular, is linked in the popular culinary mind with a frying pan and some grease. It was not always like that, however, and during colonial times in North Carolina eels were given pride of place—without being fried—on the table. New Bern's most famous building is Tryon Palace, which was built for British governor William Tryon in 1765, when New Bern was named the colonial capital. The following recipe for "eel pye with oysters," reproduced in *A Tryon Palace Trifle,* is from the palace's eighteenth-century kitchen:

Rowl your Past thin and lay it in Your Dish, then take great eels. Skin, Gutt, and cutt them in pieces, wash and dry them, then lay some Butter in Your Pye, and Season your Eels, with pepper, salt, Nutmeg, Cloves, and Mace. Cover them all over with Large Oysters and Put in 3 or 4 bay Leaves, then put in more of your Spices and Salt, then cover them well with Butter, and put in 3 or 4 Spoonfull of White Wine so close and Bake it, & Eate it hott.

Skin them, cut them into pieces, and put them into a skillet with verjuyce [acid juice of unripe grapes] and fair water as much as will cover them, some large mace, pepper, a quarter of a pound of currants, two or three onions, three or four spoonfuls of yeast, and a bundle of sweet herbs, stew all these together until the eels are very tender, then dish them, and put to the broth a quarter of a pound of butter, a little salt, and sugar, pour it on the fish and serve it hot.

As time went on, things were simplified. A good eel stew turned up in kitchens on both sides of the Atlantic all through the 1800s. A standard North Carolina version, presented in the cookbook *Coastal Carolina Cooking,* produces a simple and tasty stewed eel:

2 pounds skinned eel fillets, cut into one-inch chunks
4 medium Irish potatoes, peeled and diced
2 medium onions, chopped
2 quarts water
1 teaspoon salt
¼ teaspoon black pepper
2 tablespoons bacon drippings

In a large saucepan, add eel, diced potatoes, and chopped onions to water. Season with salt, pepper, and bacon drippings. Bring to a boil, reduce heat, and simmer 45 minutes. Serves 4.

Jellied eels are available in twenty-first-century London at stalls like Vic Hollister's in London's public street markets. But for anyone who has a skinned eel on hand, jellied eels can be fixed at home. As part of its campaign to turn eels into a major North Carolina cash crop, the Sea Grant program at the University of North Carolina put out a booklet about the harvesting, handling, and marketing of the fish, which included a simple recipe for jellied eel:

1 pound of eel, cut into one-inch pieces
    (skinning isn't necessary)
water salted at the rate of 1 teaspoon per pint
juice of one lemon
bay leaf

Put the eel, bay leaf and lemon juice into a saucepan with just
enough salted water to cover them. Cook at low heat for two
hours. Cool the cooked eel as rapidly as possible. As it cools,
the liquor should set in a jelly. Adding gelatin shouldn't be necessary.

Eat it with a strong vinegar, or a hot pepper vinegar, made
by steeping a hot pepper in a white wine vinegar.

The same source had a simple and tasty recipe for baked eel:

2 pounds of eel, skinned, cut into two-inch pieces
¼ cup olive oil
1 clove garlic, coarsely chopped
a pinch of thyme leaves
juice of ½ lemon
lemon slices
parsley

Sprinkle blended salt and pepper over the pieces of eel. Heat
the olive oil in a baking dish. Add the garlic and thyme. Place
the eel in this hot mixture, squeeze a little lemon juice over it,
and bake in a moderate oven (375°) for twenty-five to thirty
minutes. Garnish with lemon slices and parsley. Serves six.

Jane Grigson, a superb English food writer, summed her own
taste for eel up nicely in *Jane Grigson's Fish Book:* "I love eel. Sometimes I think it is my favorite fish. It is delicate, but rich; it falls
neatly from the bone; grilled to golden brown and flecked with dark

crustiness from a charcoal fire, it makes the best of all picnic food; stewed in red wine, cushioned with onions and mushrooms, bordered with triangles of fried bread, it is the meal for cold nights in autumn; smoked and cut into elegant fillets, it starts a wedding feast or a Christmas Eve dinner with style and confidence."

Bibliography

GENERAL

Bertin, Léon. *Eels.* Translated by Betty Roquerbe. London: Cleaver-Hume Press, 1956.

Bolloré, Gwenn-Aël. *La Saga de L'Anguille.* Paris: Gallimard, 1986.

Forrest, David. *Eel Capture, Culture, Processing, and Marketing.* Surrey, Eng.: Fishing News Books, 1976.

Goode, George Brown. *The Fisheries and Fishery Industries of the United States.* 8 vols. Washington: Government Printing Office, 1884.

Jacobs, Francine. *The Freshwater Eel.* New York: William Morrow, 1973.

Karakoltsidis, Pavlos A., and Spiros M. Constantinides. "The Eels, *Anguilla spp.,* Their Characteristics and Uses." *Food Reviews International* 11 (1995): 347–61.

Kurlansky, Mark. *Cod.* New York: Penguin, 1997.

Moriarty, Christopher. *Eels: A Natural and Unnatural History.* New York: Universe Books, 1978.

Profumo, David, and Graham Swift. *The Magic Wheel: An Anthology of Fishing in Literature.* London: Heinemann, 1985.

Radcliffe, William. *Fishing from the Earliest Times.* Chicago: Ares Publishers, 1974.

Root, Waverly. *Food.* New York: Simon and Schuster, 1980.

———. *The Food of Italy.* New York: Vintage Books, 1992.

Root, Waverly, and Pichard de Rochement. *Eating in America.* New York: William Morrow, 1976.

Sinha, V. R., and J. W. Jones. *The European Freshwater Eel.* Liverpool: Liverpool University Press, 1975.

Svedäng, H., et al. "Accuracy and Precision in Eel Age Estimation, Using Otoliths of Known and Unknown Age." *Journal of Fish Biology* 53 (1998): 456–64.

Tesch, Friedrich-Wilhelm. *The Eel*. Translated by Jennifer Greenwood. London: Chapman and Hall, 1977.

Trager, James. *The Food Chronology of James Trager*. New York: Henry Holt, 1995.

Trey, Robert J. de. "Eel Mops and Table Fare." *Sea Frontiers* (March–April 1988): 128.

Warner, William. *Beautiful Swimmers*. Boston: Little, Brown and Co., 1976.

Watson, Bruce. "You Gotta Remember, Eels Are Weird." *Smithsonian Magazine* (February 2000): 124–32.

Whitlock, Ralph. *Eels*. East Sussex, Eng.: Wayland Publishers, 1979.

CHAPTER I. PAMLICO COUNTY, NORTH CAROLINA

Cecelski, David. "The Wild Plums at Core Creek; Or, In Praise of Slow Cooking." *Carolina Comments* (September 1997): 121–29.

Genthe, Henry. "The Sargasso Sea." *Smithsonian Magazine* (November 1998): 82–86.

Jones, Ernest. *The Life and Work of Sigmund Freud*. New York: Basic Books, 1953.

Kusche, Lawrence David. *The Bermuda Triangle Mystery Solved*. New York: Harper and Row, 1975.

Lawson, John. *Lawson's History of North Carolina*. Richmond: Garrett and Massie Publishers, 1937.

Lembke, Janet. *River Time: Life on an American Frontier*. New York: Lyons Press, 1989.

Mason, Bill. *The Life and Times of Bill Mason*. Oriental, N.C.: published by the author, 1992.

Mobley, Joe. *Pamlico County: A Brief History*. Raleigh: North Carolina Historical Commission, 1991.

Oppian. *Halieuticks of the Nature of Fishes*. Translated by John Jones. Oxford: Oxford University, 1722.

Simpson, Bland. *Into the Sound Country: A Carolinian's Coastal Plain*. Chapel Hill: University of North Carolina Press, 1997.

Teal, John and Mildred. *The Sargasso Sea*. Boston: Little, Brown and Co., 1975.

Tsukamoto, Katsumi, and Jun Aoyama. "Evolution of Freshwater Eels of the Genus *Anguilla:* A Probable Scenario." *Environmental Biology of Fishes* 52 (1998): 139–48.

Tsukamoto, Katsumi, et al. "Do All Freshwater Eels Migrate?" *Nature* 396 (December 17, 1998): 636.

Weisenberg, Maria. "The Big Picture." An unpublished manuscript about Lucille and Billy Truitt.

Wilson, J. Larry, and David A. Turner. "Occurrence of the American Eel in the Holston River, Tennessee." *Journal of the Tennessee Academy of Science* 57 (1982): 63–64.

Winfrey, Nancy. *On Both Sides of the River.* Pamlico, N.C.: Pamlico Press, 1995.

CHAPTER 2. INTERSTATE 95

American Eel Plan Development Team. "Fishery Management Plan for the American Eel." Washington, D.C.: Atlantic States Marine Fisheries Commission, 1999.

Athletic Sports for Boys: A Repository of Graceful Recreations for Youth. New York: Dick and Fitzgerald, 1866.

Barker, Rodney. *And the Waters Turned to Blood.* New York: Simon and Schuster, 1997.

Bellamy, J. C. *Housekeeper's Guide to the Fish Market.* London: Longman, Brown, Green and Longmans, 1843.

Berg, D. R., W. R. Jones, and G. L. Crow. *The Case of the Slippery Eel.* Raleigh: University of North Carolina Sea Grant Program, 1975.

Diaby, Souleymane. "Economic Impact of Neuse River Closure on Commercial Fishing." Morehead City: North Carolina Division of Marine Fisheries, 1996.

Gibson, Kevin. "Plan Would Study, Protect American Eel." *Mystic River Press,* April 13, 2000, A-16.

Jaques, R. "A Substance from Eel Serum Producing Slow Contractions." *Nature* 175 (January 29, 1955): 212.

Jesse, Edward. *Gleanings in Natural History* (second series). London: John Murray, 1834.

Jurgensen, Karen, and Gene Crow. "The $6-Million Eel, or From Bait to

Delicacy in Four Years." *Transactions of the 42nd North American Wildlife and Natural Resources Conference* (1977): 329–35.

Sykes, Daniel P. *Migration and Development of Young American Eels, Anguilla rostrata, in Coastal North Carolina.* Raleigh: National Sea Grant Program, 1981.

CHAPTER 3. GUIPÚZCOA, BASQUE COUNTRY, SPAIN

Alvarez, Manu. "Las angulas y el besugo, por las nubes." *El Correo Español–El Pueblo Vasco,* December 19, 1983, A-8.

"Anguleros del 83: Entre el hobby y el negocio." *El Correo Español–El Pueblo Vasco,* December 17, 1983, A-6.

Arizmendiarrieta, José María. *Pensamientos.* Mondragon, Spain: Caja Laboral Popular, 1983.

Busca Isusi, José María. *Traditional Basque Cooking.* Reno: University of Nevada Press, 1987.

Eigenmann, Carl, and Clarence Hamilton Kennedy. "The Leptocephalus of the American Eel and Other American Leptocephali." *Bulletin of the United States Fish Commission* 21 (1901): 81–92.

Fricke, H., and R. Kaese. "Tracking of Artificially Matured Eels (*Anguilla anguilla*) in the Sargasso Sea and the Problem of the Eel's Spawning Site." *Naturwissenschaften* 82 (1995): 32–36.

Homer. *The Iliad.* Translated by Robert Fitzgerald. Garden City, N.Y.: Anchor Books, 1974.

Leibar, Juan. *Don José María Arizmendiarrieta y Sus Colaboradores.* Mondragon, Spain: Otalora, 1989.

McCleave, J. D. "Physical and Behavioural Controls on the Oceanic Distribution and Migration of Leptocephali." *Journal of Fish Biology* 43, Supp. A (1993): 243–73.

Morrison, Roy. *We Build the Road as We Travel.* Philadelphia: New Society Publishers, 1991.

Navaz y Sanz, José María. *Historia de una angula que se convirtió en anguila.* San Sebastián, Spain: Sociedad de Oceanografía de Guipúzcoa, 1964.

Ormaechea, José María. *The Mondragon Cooperative Experience.* Mondragon, Spain: Mondragon Corporación Cooperativa, 1991.

Pennisi, Elizabeth. "Gone Eeling." *Science News* 140 (November 9, 1991): 297–99.

——. "Much Ado about Eels." *BioScience* 39 (October 1989): 594–98.

"El precio del marisco se ha duplicado durante la semana de Navidad." *El País,* December 28, 1999, A-1.

Puerta, Elena. "El kilo de angula ronda las 11.000 pesetas." *El Diario Vasco,* December 24, 1985, A-13.

Rodriguez, Olegario, and Angeles Alvariño. *Anguilas y Angulas: Biologia, Pesca y Consuma.* Madrid: Subsecretario de la Marina Mercante, 1951.

Schmidt, Johannes. "The Breeding Places of the Eel." *The Smithsonian Report* (1924): 279–317.

Schoenfeld, Bruce. "In Pursuit of Angulas." *Saveur* (January/February 2000): 40.

Soraluce, Ramón. "Las Angulas de Aguinaga." *Euskal-Erria* 38 (January 30, 1898): 144–46.

Soyer, Alexis. *The Pantropheon.* New York: Paddington Press, 1977.

Tesch, Friedrich-Wilhelm. "Age and growth rates of North Atlantic Eel Larvae (*Anguilla* spp.), Based on Published Length Data." *Helgoländer Meeresuntersuchungen* 52 (1998): 75–83.

——. "The Sargasso Sea Eel Expedition, 1979." *Helgoländer Meeresuntersuchungen* 35 (1982): 263–77.

CHAPTER 4. LOUGH NEAGH, NORTHERN IRELAND

Andjus, R. K., et al. "Electroretinographic Evaluation of Spectral Sensitivity in Yellow and Silver Eels (*Anguilla anguilla*)." *Visual Neuroscience* 15 (1998): 923–30.

Badham, C. David. *Prose Halieutics or Ancient and Modern Fish Tattle.* London: John Parker, 1854.

Berg, T., and J. B. Steen. "Physiological Mechanisms for Aerial Respiration in the Eel." *Comparative Biochemistry and Physiology* 15 (1965): 469–84.

Beullins, K., et al. "Sex Differentiation, Changes in Length, Weight and Eye Size before and after Metamorphosis of European eel (*Anguilla anguilla* L.) Maintained in Captivity." *Aquaculture* 153 (1997): 151–62.

Buddie, J. *An Eel Hunt in the Leader.* Edinburgh: Oliver and Boyd, 1902.

Butler, D. G. "Osmoregulation in North American Eels (*Anguilla rostrata* LeSueur) on Land and in Freshwater: Effects of the Corpuscles of Stannius." *Journal of Comparative Physiology B* 169 (1999): 139–47.

Cairncross, David. *The Origin of the Silver Eel*. London: G. Shield, 1862.

Carlin, Martha, and Joel Rosenthal. *Food and Eating in Medieval Europe*. London: Hambledon Press, 1998.

Clunn, Chris. *Eels, Pie and Mash*. London: Museum of London, 1995.

Cooper, J. *The Art of Cookery*. London: R. Lowndes, 1654.

Denning, Michael. *Ireland in Conflict*. London: Hodder & Stoughton, 1990.

Dodd, George. *The Food of London*. London: Longman, Brown, Green & Longmans, 1856.

Donnelly, Daniel J. *On Lough Neagh's Shores: A Study of the Lough Neagh Fishing Community*. Galbally, County Tyrone, Northern Ireland: published by the author, 1986.

Freeman, Sarah. *Mutton and Oysters: The Victorians and Their Food*. London: Victor Gollancz, 1989.

Grass, Günter. *The Tin Drum*. Translated by Ralph Manheim. New York: Penguin, 1961.

Hammond, P. W. *Food and Feast in Medieval England*. Dover, N.H.: Alan Sutton Publishing, 1993.

Hazlitt, W. Carew. *Old Cookery Books and Ancient Cuisine*. London: Book Lover's Library, 1893.

Healy, Tim. *Stolen Waters*. London: Longmans, Green & Co., 1913.

Heaney, Seamus. *A Door Into the Dark*. London: Faber and Faber, 1969.

Helfman, Gene S. "Spinning for Their Supper." *Natural History* (May 1995): 26–29.

Helfman, Gene S., and Jennifer B. Clark. "Rotational Feeding: Overcoming Gape-Limited Foraging in Anguillid Eels." *Copeia* (1986): 679–85.

Krueger, William H., and Kenneth Oliveira. "Sex, Size and Gonad Morphology of Silver American Eels, *Anguilla rostrata*." *Copeia* (1997): 415–20.

Lamothe, Peter, et al. "Homing and Movement of Yellow-Phase

American Eels in Freshwater Ponds." *Environmental Biology of Fishes* 58 (2000): 393–99.

Marshall, Mrs. A. B. *Larger Cookery Book of Extra Recipes.* London: Marshall's School of Cookery, 1902.

Mayhew, Henry. *London Labour and the London Poor.* London: Frank Cass and Co., 1967.

Napier, Mrs. Alexander, ed. *A Noble Boke off Cookery.* London: Elliot Stock, 1882.

Plot, David. *The Natural History of Stafford-shire.* Oxford: 1686.

Smith, Jim. *Pie 'N' Mash: A Guide to Londoners' Traditional Eating Houses.* London: Pie and Mash Club, 1995.

Wichert, Sabine. *Northern Ireland since 1945.* London: Longman, 1991.

Wilson, C. Anne. *Food and Drink in Britain.* London: Constable and Co., 1973.

CHAPTER 5. YANKEE EELS

Barbin, Gayle P. "The Role of Olfaction in Homing and Estuarine Migratory Behavior of Yellow-Phase American Eels." *Canadian Journal of Fisheries and Aquatic Sciences* 55 (1998): 564–75.

Boer, Jacob de. "8-Year Study on the Elimination of PCBs and Other Organochlorine Compounds from Eel (*Anguilla anguilla*) under Natural Conditions." *Environmental Science and Technology* 28 (1994): 2242–48.

Boosey, Thomas. *Anecdotes of Fish and Fishing.* London: Hamilton, Adams, and Co., 1887.

Burolini, Helen. *Festa.* San Diego: Harcourt Brace Jovanovich, 1988.

Butler, Eva L. Unpublished papers. Old Mystic, Conn.: Indian and Colonial Research Center.

Castonguay, Martin, et al. "Distinction between American Eels (*Anguilla rostrata*) of Different Geographic Origins on the Basis of Their Organochlorine Contaminant Levels." *Canadian Journal of Aquatic Sciences* 46 (1989): 836–43.

Cole, John. "Maine's Elvers Under Threat." *Audubon* 98 (July/August 1996): 24.

Couillard, C. M., et al. "Correlations between Pathological Changes and

Chemical Contamination in American Eels, *Anguilla rostrata,* from the St. Lawrence River." *Canadian Journal of Fisheries and Aquatic Sciences* 54 (1997): 1916–27.

Fleming, Thomas. *The Pilgrims' First Years in America.* New York: W. W. Norton, 1963.

Fromme, Hermann, et al. "Levels of Synthetic Musks: Bromocyclene and PCBs in Eel (*Anguilla anguilla*) and PCBs in Sediment from Some Waters of Berlin, Germany." *Chemosphere* (1999): 1723–35.

George, Jean Craighead. *The First Thanksgiving.* New York: Philomel Books, 1993.

Glasse, Hannah. *The Art of Cookery Made Plain and Easy.* London, 1747.

Goodwin, John. *The Pilgrim Republic: An Historical Review of the Colony of New Plymouth, with Sketches of the Rise of Other New England Settlements, the History of Congregationalism, and the Creeds of the Period.* Boston: Houghton Mifflin, 1888.

Grosell, M., et al. "Cu Uptake, Metabolism and Elimination in Fed and Starved European Eels (*Anguilla anguilla*) during Adaptation to Water-Borne Cu Exposure." *Comparative Biochemistry and Physiology* Part C 120 (1998): 295–305.

Harland, Marion. *Common Sense in the Household.* New York: Scribner, Armstrong & Co., 1874.

Hazard, Thomas Robinson. *The Jonnycake Papers of "Shepherd Tom" together with Reminiscences of Narragansett Schools of Former Days.* Boston: n.p., 1918.

Jones, Evan. *American Food: The Gastronomic Story.* New York: E. P. Dutton, 1975.

Josselyn, John. *Two Voyages to New England.* Cambridge, Eng.: E. W. Metcalf and Co., 1833.

Knights, B. "Risk Assessment and Management of Contamination of Eels (*Anguilla* SPP.) by Persistent Xenobiotic Organochlorine Compounds." *Chemistry and Ecology* 13 (1997): 171–212.

McKenzie, Clyde, Jr. *The Fisheries of Raritan Bay.* New Brunswick, N.J.: Rutgers University Press, 1992.

Moore, Kirk. "'Ladder' May Help 'Ranchers' Master Eel Life Cycle, Save Crop." *Asbury Park Press,* March 1, 1998, A-3.

Moss, Kay, and Kathryn Hoffman. *The Backcountry Housewife.* Vol. 1. Gastonia, N.C.: Schiele Museum, 1994.

Sagard-Théodat, Gabriel. *The Long Journey to the Country of the Hurons.* Edited with introduction and notes by George M. Wrong and translated by H. H. Langton. Toronto: Champlain Society, 1939.

Vøllestad, Leif Asbjørn. "Geographic Variation in Age and Length at Metamorphosis of Maturing European Eel: Environmental Effects and Phenotypic Plasticity." *Journal of Animal Ecology 61* (1992): 41–48.

White, E. M., and B. Knights. "Environmental Factors Affecting Migration of the European Eel in the Rivers Severn and Avon, England." *Journal of Fish Biology* (1997): 1104–16.

Wolcott, Imogene. *The Yankee Cookbook.* New York: Coward-McCann, 1939.

Yang, H. N. "Uptake and Elimination of Cadmium by Japanese Eel, *Anguilla japonica,* at Various Temperatures." *Bulletin of Environmental Contamination and Toxicology* 56 (April 1996): 670–76.

CHAPTER 6. FISHING AND FARMING

Collins, Geneva, "Bob Caples, Eel Hunter." *Washington Post,* July 26, 2000, F-1.

Crawford, Brian. *Fishing for Big Eels.* Shropshire: Big E Publications, 1983.

Murphy, Morgan. "A Meal of Eel." *Esquire* (July 1998): 25.

Ohta, Hiromi, et al. "Artificial Fertilization Using Testicular Spermatazoa in the Japanese Eel, *Anguilla Japonica.*" *Fisheries Science* 63 (1997): 393–96.

Robichaux, Mark. "Plague of Asian Eels Highlights Damage from Foreign Species." *Wall Street Journal,* September 27, 2000, A-1.

Silva, Beth. "Emerging Eel Economics." *AgVentures* (December 1998/ January 1999): 46–51.

Spotts, Daniel. "Eel Farming in Japan." *Oceans* 18 (March 1985): 30–33.

Swasy, Alecia. "'High Anxiety' Is a Constant Problem for the Lowly Eel." *Wall Street Journal,* January 5, 1990, A-1.

Walton, Izaak, and Charles Cotton. *The Compleat Angler.* London: Oxford University Press, 1960.

Yamamoto, K., and K. Yamauchi. "Sexual Maturation of Japanese Eel Larvae in the Aquarium." *Nature* (1974): 220–21.

Yoshii, Ryuichi. *Sushi*. Boston: Periplus Editions, 1998.

A TASTE OF EEL

Davidson, Alan. *Mediterranean Seafood*. Harmondsworth, Eng.: Penguin Books, 1972.

Davidson, Alan and Jane, eds. *Dumas on Food: Selections from "Le Grand Dictionnaire de Cuisine" by Alexandre Dumas*. London: Michael Joseph, 1978.

Davis, Nancy, and Kathy Hart. *Coastal Carolina Cooking*. Chapel Hill: University of North Carolina Press, 1986.

Farrington, Doris. *Fireside Cooks and Black Kettle Recipes*. Indianapolis: Bobbs-Merrill, 1976.

Forsyth, J. S. *A Dictionary of Diet*. London: Henry Cremer, 1833.

Grigson, Jane. *Jane Grigson's Fish Book*. London: Michael Joseph, 1993.

Guy, Christian. *An Illustrated History of French Cuisine*. New York: The Orion Press, 1962.

May, Robert. *The Accomplisht Cook or the Art and Mystery of Cooking*. London: Nathaniel Brooke, 1960.

Pellugrat, Henri-Paul. *Modern French Culinary Art*. Cleveland: World Publishing Co., 1966.

Acknowledgments

First, thanks to two friends, Sue Katz and Nancy Hartzenbusch, for giving me shelter during my research. Each was kind enough to give me a welcoming hug and the keys to her home, then point me toward a library: the British Library and the Library of Congress, respectively. And, to my mother, Adele, who did the same while I used the library at Vanderbilt University. Thanks also to the Indian and Colonial Research Center in Old Mystic, Connecticut, for the chance to consult the unpublished papers of Eva L. Butler. In addition, Janet Lembke was kind enough to provide me with information about classical Greece.

Thanks are also, obviously, due to all those who consented to be interviewed for this book. Without their patience, it would not have been written. And, for a variety of other kinds of assistance, thanks to José Manuel Álvarez Flórez, Tomohiro Asakawa, Bill Bemis, Theodore Bestor, Daniel Capella, Luisa and Vincenzo d'Arista, Carlos Guàrdia, Bridget and Susan Hale-Vranckx, Esther Jones, Andrée and Alan LeQuire, Molly Manier, Carmen Martínez Gómez, Terry Mollner, David Raper, the Sawyers (Katie, E. T. and Loyd), and Chris Wilson.

Index

African Americans, as fishermen, 8

Aguinaga, Spain, xiii, 56–68 passim, 77

Albertus Magnus: *Book of Animals,* 73, 101–2

Albufera, 67, 68, 150

American Century Cookbook, 121

American eels (*Anguilla rostrata*), 15, 16–17, 42, 44, 45, 47, 147, 154

American Heritage Cookbook and Illustrated History of American Eating and Drinking, 121

Angler's Cookbook, 134

Anguilla anguilla. See European eel

Anguilla Fish Farms, 149

Anguilla japonica. See Japanese eel

Anguilla rostrata. See American eel

Antiphanes, 69–70

Arapahoe, N.C., xiii, 7, 31, 36, 54, 150

Aristophanes: *Lysistrata,* 69

Aristotle, xii; *Natural History,* 12, 13, 71–72, 73

Arizmendiarrieta, José María, 63, 64–65

Asian swamp eels, 102

Athletic Sports for Boys, 53

Avault, James, 67

Bach: *The Natural History of East and West Prussia,* 102

Badham, C. David: *Prose Halieutics or Ancient and Modern Fish Tattle,* 89–90

Bait: for eels, 26, 137–38; eels as, 26, 129–31, 132

Baked eel, recipe for, 158

Bann River, 81, 82, 109, 135

Basques, 57, 58, 61–62, 68; cuisine of, 77–79

Bears, 28–30, 32

Beck, Horace: *The Folklore of Maine,* 136–37

Belhaven, N.C., 26, 37

Bellamy, J. C.: *Housekeeper's Guide to the Fish Market,* 38

Berners, Dame Juiliana: *A Treatyse of Fysshynge with an Angle,* 138

Bertin, Léon: *Eels: A Biological Study,* 99, 144

Billingsgate Fish Market (London), 90, 97–99, 116

Bioaccumulation, 124
Bokelaar, Mirella, 148
Bokelaar, Willy, 36, 43, 147–48, 149
Book of St. Albans, 138
Bosse, Maurice, 37
Bosse, Wilhelmina, 37
Bouw, Marie, 32–41 passim, 53–54, 125
Bouw, Martie, 31–44 passim, 52, 53–55, 79, 112, 129, 131, 147, 151
Braddy, Ann, 26–28, 31, 37
Braddy, Wayne, 27
Brooks, Albert, 133–34, 137
Bruño, Andres, 60–61

Cantabrian Sea, 57, 77
Cape May, N.J., 147
Capitone, 122
Catfish, 39, 113, 121, 141; walking, 102
Cephisus River, 69
Chapel Market (London), 91–92, 93
Chesapeake Bay, 7, 35, 140
China, 17, 42, 56, 79, 80
Chocowinity, N.C., 48
Chocowinity Bay, 48, 49
Claus, Carl, 14
Coastal Carolina Cooking, 157
Cod, 57, 80, 96, 114, 116, 121
Collard greens, recipe for, 154–55
Colonists, New World, xii, 19, 20, 114–16, 117
Columbus, Christopher, 18, 57

Concise Encyclopedia of Gastronomy, 156
Conger eels, 68
Connecticut, 43, 118, 133, 137
Consumption of eels: in colonial America, xii, 19, 113–14, 115–16, 117; European, 17, 21, 31, 54, 80, 82, 111, 112, 113, 116, 143, 148, 149–50, 156–57; Japanese, 17, 41, 42, 65, 79, 143, 144–45, 146, 147, 156; English, 20, 66, 89, 95–97, 157, 158–59; in North Carolina, 20–21, 157–58; U.S., 21, 31, 111–12, 113, 117–19, 120, 121, 122–23, 130, 137, 141, 148, 154, 155; French, 21, 96; German, 32, 54, 116, 122, 156; Italian, 32–33, 116, 121, 122, 133; Dutch, 54, 89, 116, 156; Spanish, 65, 66–67, 68, 77–79, 150; Chinese, 65, 91; by ancient Celts, 66; by ancient Romans, 68; Greek, 69–71; in London, 89–91, 92, 93–95, 98; by Native Americans, 116–17, 120; Polish, 121, 122, 133
Costermongers, 98–99
Crabs, 7, 10, 11–12, 18, 19, 23, 27, 45, 121; as bait, 26, 123
Craven County, N.C., 6, 7–8
Crawford, Brian: *Fishing for Big Eels,* 139
Crèvecouer, J. Hector St. John de: *Letters from an American Farmer,* 123

Dams, 46, 123
DDT, 45, 128
Defoe, Daniel: *Tour of Great Britain,* 66
Delaware Valley Seafood, 37, 111, 112, 113, 129, 131
Development, land, 45–47
Dioxins, 45
Dodd, George: *The Food of London,* 97
Domesday Book, 19–20
Dowdeswell, Peter, 66
Dumas, Alexandre: *Grand Dictionnaire de Cuisine,* 69, 156

East Carolina University: Institute for Coastal and Marine Resources, 142
Eel and pie shops, 94–95
Eelers: U.S., 37–38, 39, 48, 50–51, 129, 132; Basque, 58–61, 65; Northern Irish, 83, 84, 85, 88–89; Native American, 135, 136
Eeling, 12, 48, 86–88, 115, 118, 132–41; winter, 123, 133, 136–37; accidental, 139–40, 141. *See also* Fisheries
Eel pie, 95, 96, 99, 133; with oysters, recipe for, 155
Eel Pie House (London), 95
Eel River, 115
Eels: life cycle/development of, xi, 12–13, 15–16, 41, 73, 99, 127–28, 146, 152, 153; and pollutants/water quality, 10–11, 43–45, 49, 60, 67, 68, 123–24, 125, 127, 128, 150; use of pots for catching, 12, 26, 27, 36, 48, 49–50, 51, 116, 125, 130, 132, 133, 136, 151; sliminess of, 13–14, 53, 101, 105, 134; sex of, 17, 43, 52–53, 99–100; transportation of, 25–26, 31, 32, 33, 35, 40, 79, 97, 122, 130–31, 133; storage tanks for, 31, 32, 37, 52–53, 129, 131, 147, 148, 150; and water temperature, 44; respiration of, 46, 101, 134, 137; overcrowding among, 47, 100; cannibalism among, 47, 104–5, 142; diet of, 50, 83–84, 101–4, 105, 127, 128, 138, 142, 143, 146, 148, 150–51; habitat of, 68–69, 103, 105, 152–53; worship of, 69–70; weirs as method for catching, 82, 109, 135–36; age range of, 99; hibernation by, 103, 123, 133, 152; predators of, 104; defenses of, 105; sense of smell of, 125–26; angling as method for catching, 138–41. *See also* American eels; Bait; Consumption of eels; Eelers; Eeling; Elvers; European eels; Farming, eel; Fisheries; Japanese eels; Larvae, eel; Migration of eels; Reproduction, eel; Silver eels; Yellow eels
Eel stew, recipes for, 156–57
Egypt, 69–70, 74

Eigenmann, Carl, 74

El Palmar, Spain, xi, 150

Elvers, 41, 99; appearance and development of, 15; defined, 15; migration of, 15, 44, 46–47, 68, 81–82, 101, 109, 125; import/export of, 42, 56, 79–80, 81, 82, 146–47; and farming, 42, 142, 145, 146; decrease of in Europe, 47, 79, 81; consumption of, 65, 66–67, 77–79, 145; etymology of term, 66; transportation of, 82, 109, 133; ladders for, 109, 126–27. *See also* Fisheries—elver

England, 17, 56, 66, 139; eel fisheries in, 19–20, 136; eel consumption in, 20, 66, 89, 95–97, 157, 158–59. *See also* London, England

European eels (*Anguilla anguilla*), 15, 16–17, 42, 147, 156

European Inland Fishery Advisory Committee, 75

European Union (EU), 56, 61, 79–80, 149; Scientific, Technical, and Economic Committee for Fisheries (STECF), 79

Euskadi Ta Askatasuna (ETA), 61, 62, 83

Evesham Abbey, 19–20

Farming, eel, 141–42; in Japan, 17, 41, 42, 143, 145, 146; in Europe, 21, 41, 80, 91, 113, 141, 149, 156;

in China, 41, 42, 65, 79, 147, 149; in Taiwan, 42; in North Carolina, 143, 148; in Florida, 149; in Spain, 149–51

Fisheries

—eel: U.S., 19, 31, 47–48, 120; English, 19–20, 136; European, 21, 37; in North Carolina, 26, 27, 35–36, 37, 48–49, 51; Canadian, 35, 124–25; exhaustion of, 36, 47, 49, 144; Spanish, 68, 150; Northern Irish, 83–84, 85, 86–88, 110; rights to, 84, 85; Italian, 102–3; Native American, 116; in New Jersey, 123; in New York, 123–24; Japanese, 144, 145

—elver: U.S., 42–43; and prohibitions, 43, 56, 79–80, 146, 147, 148; in North Carolina, 43, 146; exhaustion of, 47, 79, 146; Spanish, 58–61, 67, 68, 79; French, 61, 80; English, 66; Italian, 66; Northern Irish, 81–82, 109; Japanese, 144, 146; in New Jersey, 146–47

Florida, 43, 102

Form of Cury, 20

France, 21, 61, 66, 70, 96, 135, 147

Franco, Francisco, 62–63, 64

Franquesa, Ramon, 80

Freud, Sigmund, 14, 73

Fulton Fish Market (New York City), 97, 121–23, 133

Gallagher, Margie, 142–43, 152
Germany, 32, 54, 116, 122
Glass eels. *See* Elvers
Goode, George Brown, xiv, 102,
    120, 123–24
Goodwin, John: *The Pilgrim Repub-
    lic,* 115
Gookin, Daniel: *Historical Account
    of the Indians,* 116–17
Grass, Günther: *The Tin Drum,*
    103–4
Great American Seafood Cookbook,
    121
Greece, 45, 69–70, 71
Grigson, Jane: *Jane Grigson's Fish
    Book,* 158–59
Guipúzcoa Province (Spain),
    56–57, 62
Gula, 78–79
Gulf Stream, 144

Harland, Marion: *Common Sense in
    the Household,* 120
Hawkins, Jess, 35–36
Hazard, Thomas Robinson: *The
    Jonnycake Papers,* 118–19
Heaney, Seamus: "A Lough
    Neagh Sequence," 87–88
Herodotus, 69
Herring, 50–51
Hogs, farming of, 44–45, 49
Holland, 54, 89, 116, 156
Holland Seafood, 32, 33, 36, 37,
    43, 52, 53, 112, 113, 129, 147, 151
Hollister, Vic, 91, 92–93, 94, 157

Homer: *Iliad,* 70
Hopkins, Dick, 129–31, 132
Hurricane Floyd, 10, 11, 44–45
Hutchinson, Helen, 48
Hutchinson, Robert, 48–49

International Council for the
    Exploration of the Sea, 75
International Investigations of
    the Sea, 74
Ireland, 79, 99. *See also* Northern
    Ireland
Irish Republican Army (IRA), 82,
    85
Irish Sea, 73, 81, 82
Italy, 32–33, 66, 102–3, 116

Japan: eel consumption in, 17,
    41, 42, 65, 79, 143, 144–45, 146,
    147, 156; eel farming in, 17, 41,
    42, 143, 145, 146; eel/elever
    fisheries in, 144, 145, 146
Japanese eels (*Anguilla japonica*),
    40–41, 65, 143–44, 145, 146,
    147
Jellied eels, 90–91, 92, 93, 157;
    recipe for, 157–58
Jenrick, Mick, 90–91, 92, 93
Jesse, Edward: *Gleanings in Natural
    History,* 46
Johnston, Patrick, 86–87, 88
"Josephines." *See* Mullet
Josselyn, Henry: *Two Voyages to
    New England,* 115–16
Josselyn, John, 115

Joy of Cooking, 121
Juvenal, 68–69

Kabayaki, 65, 145, 146, 147, 148
Kaup (German naturalist), 73
Kennedy, Clarence, 74
Kennedy, Oliver, 81–89 passim,
    106, 109–10
Kils, Uwe, 126–29, 152
Koonce, Gary, 49–51, 52, 104, 112
Korea, 42, 144
Kratchman, Barry, 39, 111–13, 129,
    131, 146–47
Kratchman, David, 112
Kratchman, Sheldon, 113
Kuroshio current, 42, 144

Lake Comacchio, 66, 102–3, 116
Larousse Gastronomique, 146
Larrañaga, Juan Antonio, 58–60
Larvae, eel, 72; migration of, xi,
    15, 41, 42, 77, 100–101, 143–
    44; transformation of, xi, 74,
    75; hatching of, 15, 16, 145; re-
    search on, 73–75, 145–46; diet
    of, 146
Lawson, John, 20, 29; *A New
    Voyage to Carolina,* 20
Leeuwenhoek, Antonie van, 73
Leptocephali. *See* Larvae, eel
Linnaeus, Carolus, 73
Loire River, 61, 66, 80, 135, 147
London, England, 84, 89–99
    passim, 116, 157
Longshan, 149

Lough Neagh, 81–82, 83; eel/elver
    fisheries on, 81–89, 106–10
Lough Neagh Fishermen's Co-
    operative Society, 81, 85, 88, 91,
    106, 135
Lough Neagh flies, 83–84, 107
Lukas, Tiburcio Eskisabel, 78–79,
    95

McCleave, James, 76–77, 100, 106
McElroy, Bill, 106, 107–8, 109–10
McKenzie, Clyde: *The Fisheries of
    Raritan Bay,* 123
Maine, 43, 115, 136–37
Manze's Eel and Pie House (Lon-
    don), 94
Maryland, 19, 31, 37, 122
Mason, Billy, 25
Mataro, 71
Matelote, recipe for, 156
May, Robert, 156–57; *The Accom-
    plisht Cook, or the Art and Mystery
    of Cookery,* 96
Mayhew, Henry: *London Labour
    and the London Poor,* 98, 99
Menagier de Paris, 96
Merrimac River, 118, 123–24
Midgyett, George, 25
Migration of eels: xi, xii, 15, 16,
    18, 61, 76–77, 99, 100, 101, 151–
    52, 153; overland, 46–47, 101.
    See also Elvers: migration of;
    Larvae, eel: migration of
Mondini, Carlo: *De Anguillae
    Ovariis,* 73

Mondragon, Spain, 62, 63–64
Moriarty, Christopher: *Eels: A Natural and Unnatural History,* 66, 99
Morris, William, 73
Mosquitoes, 127, 128
Mullet, 7, 8, 10, 11, 12, 22
Mystic River, 133, 134

Narragansett Bay, 133
National Marine Fisheries Service (NMFS), 47
Native Americans, 114, 115, 116–17, 120
Netherlands. *See* Holland
Neuse River, 7, 20, 36, 44–45, 50
New Bern, N.C., 5–6, 7, 155
New Jersey, 123, 126–27, 146–47
New York, N.Y., 121, 123
Nile River, 69
Noble Boke off Cookery, 20
North Carolina, 5–12, 22–30; eel sales in, 19, 31; eel consumption in, 20–21, 157–58; eel/elver fisheries in, 26, 27, 35–36, 37, 38, 43, 48–49, 51, 146; eel farming in, 143, 148
North Carolina Division of Marine Fisheries, 35–36
North East River, 39
Northern Ireland, 135; sectarian conflict in, 61, 82–83, 106–7; eel/elver fisheries in, 81–82, 83–84, 85, 86–89, 109, 110
North Sea, 106

Oppian, 13, 14; *Halieuticks of the Nature of Fishes,* 137
Organochlorines, 124, 125
Oria River, 56, 57, 59, 60, 68, 147
Oriental, N.C., 7, 9, 22–32 passim, 48
Orio, Spain, 57–58, 59
Otamendi, Santiago, 67

Pamlico County, N.C., 5–12, 20–30
Pamlico River, 7, 32, 36, 48, 50
Pamlico Sound, 7, 9, 22, 26, 27, 32, 49
Pepys, Samuel, 68
Pettaquamscutt River, 118
Philadelphia, Pa., 31–33, 37, 111–12
Philetaerus, 69
Pie and mash shops, 94–95
Piers of Fulham, 20
Pine Barrens (New Jersey), 127
Pliny the Elder, 13
Pollution. *See* Water quality
Polychlorinated biphenyls (PCBs), 45, 123, 124, 125
Putte, 99

Radcliffe, William: *Fishing from the Earliest Times,* 68
Randolph, Mary: *The Virginia Housewife,* 119–20
Raritan Bay, 123
Redi, Francesco, 66
Reproduction, eel, 14–15, 16, 18, 61, 73, 100, 120, 153; mysteries

of, xiv, 14, 71–73, 75; organs
    of, 14, 72–73; in captivity, 17;
    and sexual development, 17,
    100; and sperm and eggs, 75;
    and hermaphroditism, 100; and
    artificial fertilization, 145
Rhode Island, 117–18, 130, 132–33
Ring (eel dealing consortium), 84,
    85
Roanoke River, 50–51
Robberecht, George, 35, 37
Romans, 68
Root, Waverly, 117; *Food,* 70
Roots, William, xii–xiii
Rutgers Institute of Marine and
    Coastal Sciences, 126
Ryuku Trench, 144

St. Lawrence River, 45, 124–25
Salmon, 12–13, 100
Samoset, 114
San Sebastián, Spain, 56, 62, 67,
    77, 78
Sargasso Sea, xi, 14–15, 16, 19, 41,
    54, 55, 68, 82, 84, 99, 100, 106,
    124, 144, 151, 153; description
    of, 17–18; research in, 75–77
Sashimi, 65
Schmidt, Johannes, 15, 16, 41;
    research of, 74–75, 146
Sea Grant, 35, 36, 157
Settlement Cookbook, 121
Severn River, 19–20, 66, 81, 145,
    147
Shrimp, 7, 26, 45, 93

Silver eels, 99, 115, 117, 124, 125;
    defined, 16
Simmons, Amelia: *American
    Cookery,* 118
Slavin, Herb, 121, 122
Smoked eel, 32, 54, 65, 116, 117,
    156
South Carolina, 43
Spain, 17, 56, 66; Basque re-
    gion of, 56–65 passim, 77, 83;
    eel/elver fisheries in, 58–61, 67,
    68, 79, 150; eel consumption in,
    65, 66–67, 68, 77–79, 150; eel
    farming in, 149–51
Spallanzani, Lazare, 102–3
Squanto. *See* Tisquantum
Stark, William, 124
Stewed eels, recipes for, 156–57
Surimi, 78
Sushi, 65, 145
Sybaris, 71
Syracuse, 70–71
Syrski, Szymon, 73

Tesch, Friedrich-Wilhelm: *Der
    Aal,* 75, 125–26; research of,
    75–76
Thoreau, Henry David, 118, 124
Tisquantum, 114–15, 136
Toomebridge, Northern Ireland,
    xiii, 81
Torres, Juan, 149–51
Trash fish, 10, 26, 78, 141
Truitt, Billy, 8–11, 22, 24, 25, 30,
    151

Truitt, Lucille Styron, 8, 21–26, 31, 151; one-pot collard greens recipe of, 154–55
Tryon, William, 155
Tryon Palace Trifle, 155
Tsukiji market (Tokyo), 97

United States: eel/elver fisheries in, 19, 31, 42–43, 47–48, 120; eel consumption in, 21, 31, 111–12, 113, 117–19, 120, 121, 122–23, 130, 137, 141, 148, 154, 155. *See also specific states*
U.S. Department of Agriculture, 140
U.S. Department of Commerce, 47
U.S. Department of Fisheries, 120
University of Maine, 76
Uranga, Ramon, 59

Valencia, Spain, xi, 67, 68, 149, 150

Virginia, 19, 31, 37, 119–20, 122, 148

Walton, Izaak: *The Compleat Angler,* 138
Water quality, 10–11, 43–45, 49, 60, 67, 68, 123–24, 125, 127, 128, 150
Weyerhauser Paper Company, 51–52
Whiteside, Dugan, 149
Willis, Lionel, 151–52
Willis, Seth, 151
Wilson, C. Anne: *Food and Drink in Britain,* 136
Wolcott, Imogene: *The Yankee Cookbook,* 117
Wood, William: *New Englands Prospect,* 116
Wychert, Billy, 48

Yellow eels, 115; defined, 16